LAWRENCE CLARK POWELL

ISLANDS

OF

Books

LOS ANGELES
DAWSON'S BOOK SHOP
1991

ISBN 0-87093-276-4

TO
WILL ROBINSON
IN
GRATITUDE AND AFFECTION

Contents

Preface

PUBLISHED for the first and only time forty
years ago, *Islands of Books* has become the
scarcest of my books. Of the thousand copies
printed by the Ward Ritchie Press, one
hundred fifty were reserved for members of
the Zamorano Club. Most of the chapters
appeared first in the club's *Hoja Volante*. A
pre-publication price of $3.00 rose later to
$4.00.

Once again is acknowledged my debt to
W. W. Robinson, the book's dedicatee, for
the writing and publication of the essays in
the quarterly he edited. He was an unlikely
midfather to these literary exercises and the
club a dubious patron, so partial was it then
to history.

As historian of the Title Insurance and
Trust Co., the city's largest, and author of
Land in California and *Ranchos Become
Cities*, Will Robinson was known as a poet
to only a few of us. His volume, *Urgent
Shapes*, appeared during the Depression
when he and his artist wife Irene lived in
Laguna Beach. They were also the authors
of a popular series of animal books for children, published by Macmillan, which he
wrote and she illustrated. When he discovered that the only sure way of making a liv-

ing was with the title company, his hope
ended for a literary career.

It was through me, as I walked the tight-
rope between literature and librarianship,
that Robinson experienced a vicarious fulfilment. It was he who urged me to write these
essays. We first met in 1934 when I was
Zeitlin's bibliofactotum. Jake's publication
of my book on Jeffers brought Robinson into
the shop to buy one of the first copies. On a
visit to Carmel in 1929, he had met Jeffers
and been photographed by Edward Weston.
That master did not fail to see the hidden
poet in his Byronic portrait of Will.

We were friends from our first meeting
until his death, sharing dreams and hopes
while we presented blank faces to our colleagues. We became Zamoranons a year
apart, he in 1942 and I a year earlier, and
when he was named editor of the club's
periodical, he sought a regular contribution
from me on any subject as long as it was
literary. We agreed that the club suffered
from literary anemia, peopled as it was with
lawyers, bankers and doctors.

His encouragement helped keep my creative gifts alive. Library work then was
sterile. When *Islands of Books* appeared in
1951 one librarian was said to have classified
it as Marine Geography! The Library of
Congress added an explanatory note on its 3
x 5 card which read *Essays*. Where did that
odd title come from other than the chapter
of the same name? I'm not sure. It was a long

dry summer and perhaps I was heat crazed. That's what I told those who asked.

Robinson and I went on to other collaborations. One of the happiest wedded history, literature and Irene's art in *The Malibu* (1958), printed at the Plantin Press by Saul and Lillian Marks. Some judge it to be the most beautiful book ever to appear in Southern California. It was not the first nor the last of my books to bear the Dawson imprint. My association with the Ward Ritchie Press also flourished. *Islands of Books* ranks as one of Ward's most engaging of the hundreds of volumes he designed.

Will Robinson was always ready to serve the public good — at the Southwest Museum, the two California historical societies and the Westerners. His authority as a land and title expert widened to include Los Angeles in its many aspects. When we founded the Friends of the UCLA Library, he was its first president.

To the end of his life, which came suddenly in 1972 at age 81, ours was a fond and fruitful relationship. We sometimes jested as to who would be the first to eulogize the other, even practiced a few times. Mine alas was the sad lot to speak at his memorial.

Fifty years were to pass from when in the 1940s, Will Robinson perceived what, in 1990, Kevin Starr has documented in his multi-volume cultural history of California, that *Islands of Books* and then *California Classics* were the first to emphasize the bond between the region's literature and its geography.

If my book laments a lost landscape, what has happened since only deepens that feeling. The essay "Personal Landscape" was written as we were packing to leave for England. As president of the California Library Association in 1949–50, I had spoken in every part of the Golden State. A grass roots movement was seeking to draft me as the next State Librarian. It would have meant leaving UCLA when we returned from the year abroad. I was already feeling pulled apart. Hence the elegiac mood of spring 1950 when the final essays were written.

Crossing the Atlantic eastward in the *Queen Elizabeth*, I worked in a deck chair on the manuscript for the Ritchie press. As we returned ten months later aboard the freighter *American Scientist*, the proofs were with me. *Islands of Books* was my first book of essays and in some ways is my favorite of all I have written, for it was in it that I found my true voice.

Now it is good to have it back in print. Although the price of this paperback is triple that of the original hardback, it is still a bargain on today's inflated market. But then I'm prejudiced.

L.C.P.

Tucson
Bajada of the
Santa Catalinas

ISLANDS OF BOOKS

The Time,
The Place, and The Book

THERE IS a power in certain books to evoke
the time and the place of their first reading, when by merely giving a glimpse of
their backs they take us backward to that
time of discovery which now seems magi-
cally inevitable. One evening I took my
younger son to the nearby branch of the
Public Library, and while he was making
his selections I glanced at the shelves of
juvenile fiction. One title transfixed me; it
was *The Rock of Chickamauga* by Joseph
A. Altsheler; and straightway I was back
in my own boyhood when, in the South
Pasadena Public Library, I devoured Altsheler's scores of books—the Civil War, the
Texan, the Border series—and hungered
for more.

After dinner I would bicycle to the Library, with a string-bag hanging from the
handlebars, and tarry only long enough to
fill it with books I had not yet read. What
a shock of pleasure it was to discover an
Altsheler new to me, then pedal home
swiftly downhill to the orange-groved

southeastern part of town, hurry up to the sleeping-porch, and go to bed with the books and a candybar! *Quelle volupté*! Sound of insects against the screen, chuckle of owls in the oaks, fragrance of the flowering pittosporum, taste of slowly dissolving chocolate on my tongue, all experienced unconsciously then in the background of the immediate excitement of the stories, but evoked with nostalgia long years after by the sight of a rebound book on a library shelf. In the wisdom that comes with the years, I no more than looked at the back of the book, risking no sample of what once was deathless prose.

Then there are poems which seem to have been written just for the occasion in which one finds himself, such as Rupert Brooke's sonnet "The Hill," beginning

Breathless we flung us on the windy hill,
Laughed in the sun and kissed the lovely grass.

Back of the college stood such a hill, green in spring with windswept oats, stalked by mustard, stemmed with brodea, all burned tawny by summer and much too stickery to do any flinging down in. On that hill, above the rosy-tiled roofs of the campus, we first read those fourteen lines, ending

Proud we were and laughed that had such
    brave true things to say—
And then you suddenly cried and turned away.

Never do I see *Lady Chatterley* on my shelf without recalling my first chance reading of Lawrence's erotic masterpiece. I read it hurriedly in one sitting in the cab of a delivery truck parked on a camphor-lined street in Oak Knoll. I had been sent out by the bookstore for which I worked to deliver a copy of the Florentine first edition to a millionaire customer of uncertain age. He had to wait for it until late in the afternoon. Now I own several editions of the book, as well as the original correspondence relating to its publication; yet my predominant memory is of that first, clandestine reading, when I ignored the basic maxim of all delivery boys' rise to success: be prompt!

Although I had read Robinson Jeffers in college, in copies belonging to Ward Ritchie, it was not until I sat up all night in a cabin in the Carmel pinewood and read *Cawdor* aloud to Gordon Newell while he carved away on a redwood ceiling-beam, and toward dawn walked with him to Mission Point and saw Tor House and Hawk Tower in the light of a gibbous moon—it was not until then that I felt compelled to study Jeffers' entire work and try to arrive at a reasonable basis for my intuitive feeling that here was poetry nearly as lasting as the granite which it adored.

I have never had such a conviction about Conrad Aiken, but I do cherish a copy of his *Selected Poems* which Fay sent me when I was in France. It accompanied me on a solitary pilgrimage to the Romanesque basilica at Vézelay whence St. Bernard had preached the Second and Third Crusades. My inn was the Cheval Blanc, my dinners were of steak and watercress, moistened by wine of the region; and afterwards I sat through the long twilights, overlooking the square, and savored poems of music and sorrow.

> While the blue noon above us arches
> And the poplar sheds disconsolate leaves,
> Tell me again why love bewitches
> And what love gives.

My fortune's nadir was reached later in a most unfortunate place to suffer fiscal depression—the French Riviera. One decisive afternoon I took the bus from the fishing village into Nice, and spent nearly all my remaining capital for a third-class ticket back to Dijon. That left me with fifty cents, ten of which were needed for bus fare. The remaining forty I invested in a paper-bound copy of Katherine Mansfield's Journal. Back on the beach I sat out of the wind with my back against a rowboat and read such poignant entries, some of which had been written in the very village where I was, as made me thankful for my own good health and indifferent to my lack of money.

I read Shelley in college—was I not an English major?—but now the sight of the dark blue Oxford text on my shelf recalls a summer afternoon in a cherry orchard on the edge of Dijon, where I lolled in a little pavilion and read Shelley, while my industrious friend Matruchot picked buckets of cherries. It was one of those great days of Burgundian summer, the golden limestone bearing its burden of vines up to the vintage, a blue sky flocked with clouds, and I perfectly convinced that

The One remains, the many change and pass;
Heaven's light forever shines, Earth's shadows
    fly;
Life, like a dome of many-coloured glass,
Stains the white radiance of Eternity.

Thus often for me have the time and the place conspired to make a book memorable. Yet increasingly am I urged to fabricate my own memorial of an intensely experienced place, even though humbly, as in these lines from an overland narrative unknown to Wagner-Camp:

"Aboard the Chief—Galesburg—4 p.m. —snowing! Weather grayed as we left Chicago and the snow began to blow like bullets by the window. Now at this flag-stop the flakes swirl softly down. I pause repeatedly from reading and writing to stare at the winter landscape. Sight of myself as a boy in an open doorway, watching the limited streak by. Later—Fort Madison— snowing harder—just crossed the Missis- sippi, creeping over the mile-wide bridge, above the slow-flowing, ice-filled river. Softly still the small flakes fall, soft yet ur- gent, and the red-and-yellow Diesel horns impatiently for the signal. At last we move. Mississippi of my life, bear me gently to my ocean!"

Nine by Nine

SOMEWHERE in his notebooks Leonardo observed that small rooms are best because they discipline the mind. I have proved for myself the truth of his dictum. My study measures 9 by 9. I have had to select everything in it—desk, three chairs, two lamps, radio, filing cabinet, two sectional wall bookcases and one under-the-window case, pictures (thirty-five assorted sizes), and the books (about a thousand) which bring the room to life. On the wall in back of my easy chair hangs the room's motto, etched for me in brass by Harold Doolittle, an exhortation from Cobden-Sanderson's Journal: *Sweet God, souse me in literature*!

Ten years ago, when we lived in the canyon, my study measured 9 by 12. It was almost completely lined with shelves which held my total private library of 1500 volumes. Now I own twice as many, in spite of constant discarding (to my college library), and the smaller room will hold only part of my books. This compels me to discipline my tastes and to choose for roommates only those volumes which I feel that I must see every day.

Note that I said "see" every day, not necessarily read. For next best to reading books is to sit at slippered ease and look at their backs. Each speaks to me in a different voice, each is fastened to my imagination by an invisible cord, and a mere glance nourishes me with the juice they hold. Instantly I recall the entire history of my relationship with each volume—when and where I acquired it, my first reading and subsequent samplings, travels it has gone with me; and when a book no longer nourishes me without my even opening it, I want no more to keep it in my study and it is either discarded or shelved elsewhere.

Only two of my childhood books have thus remained alive for me to this day; they are the first books I can remember reading—*Grimm's Fairy Tales* and Stevenson's *Home Book of Verse*. They do not travel with me, but I should not want to be long removed from them, and my heirs would do well to bury them with me.

I have always been reconciled to the fact that I was born a bibliomaniac, never have I sought a cure, and my dearest friends have been drawn from those likewise suffering from book-madness. Why should I waste the meager hours of my life staring at cinema or television, dealing in cards, fingering checker or chessman, when I can sit in the corner of my study and look with

love at the backs of my books knowing
that my wife and sons are with me under
the same roof, that my work awaits me in
the morning; and that when my eyes blur
I can go out of doors to our terraced garden, kneel on the earth and pull weeds until my hands hurt.

For next to books and man I love the
earth best; to work the soil, to saw wood
and split it and later see and feel and
smell it burn; or to stand at my window
and watch the day begin or end, the Santa
Monicas to the north, Baldwins to the
south, and on windy smogless days clear
beyond City Hall and Coliseum to the
Whittier hills. Across the way dwells the
Kite Man, a nocturnal worker with day-
time free for his hobby of building and flying kites. Sometimes he has aloft a dozen
of his constructions, motionless or dancing
in the sky, big and little flyers of several
colors and shapes, all joyfully married to
the loving wind.

Only a few unfilled inches remain on
the third and last shelf of my under-the-
window case in which I keep little books.
Within the next year, if I keep on acquir-
ing more, the case will be full, and I shall
have to review its contents and see whether
any can be discarded or shelved elsewhere.
Nearly an entire shelf is devoted to a collection of Greek lyric and pastoral poetry.
This is one of my few college-day passions

which has not cooled. It was kindled by that nonpareil teacher, poet and translator, C. F. McIntyre, and is cornerstoned by the Loeb *Greek Anthology*, *Lyra Graeca*, *Daphnis and Chloe*, and *Bucolic Poets*.

On the shelf below is a clutch of Chinese poetry in translation, also inspired by McIntyre, and which includes Waley, Waddell, Gautier, Bynner, Payne, and Pound, and of recent acquisition, Olive Percival's copy of Obata's *Li Po*.

Close by is my favorite book of the 1890's —John Gray's *Silverpoints*, exquisitely designed by Charles Ricketts as a tall, narrow octavo. Published a decade earlier was *Silverpoints*' shelfmate, *Rose Leaf and Apple Leaf* by Rennell Rodd, printed in brown on Philadelphia banknote paper, interleaved with blank green tissue, and immortalized by Wilde's royal-purple *Envoi*.

On the shelf nearest to my easy chair are the works of Peter Lum Quince, increased to four volumes by the equinoctial appearance of *A Few More*. It will probably be many years before my variorum edition of Quince is completed. The poet's longevity and revived productivity retard my work. No librarian is ever really happy until the dates on his catalog cards are finally closed. Few authors cause such delay as, for example, did "Cole, Cornelius, 1822-1924."

The next book my hand touches is bound in red linen with a red leather label and is not printed. It is a photostatic negative copy made, the stamp says, on May 1, 1943, by the Yale University Library; and the reason why I cherish it more than a gondola of Grabhorns is because—

Once upon a time in the halcyon thirties when I was domiciled in Dijon, I heard a symphony broadcast from Paris, during which a mezzo-soprano sang a suite of songs, with words by François Mauriac. For some reason those poems set to music haunted me, and through the years I sought to locate the work of Mauriac, *Orages*, from which they were taken—a privately printed edition of 200 copies dated 1925. The quest led finally to New Haven. François Mauriac is best known for his novels, and *Orages* is perhaps his only book of verse. "*Les derniers grondements d'une jeunesse qui s'éloigne*," his epigraph reads, and as I broach my forties I realize poignantly what he meant.

Mauriac writes of the pine-rocky heath around Bordeaux, a land similar to mine, where in summertime the sun goes berserk; and it was this kinship of land and weather which I sensed that distant day, when through the headlocked earphones I heard a woman's voice sing

LE CORPS FAIT ARBRE

Le parfum de ta robe attire les abeilles,
Plus que les fruits mangés que ta sandale broie.
Accueillons cet élan de végétale joie,
Ce silence de la campagne où Pan sommeille.

Rêve que désormais immobile, sans âge,
Les pieds enracinés et les mains étendues,
Tu laisses s'agiter aux orageuses nues
Une chevelure odorante de feuillage.

Les guêpes voleront sur toi sans que s'émeuve
L'écorce de ta chair où la cigale chante,
Et ton sang éternel sera, comme les fleuves,
La circulation de la terre vivante.

"Body into Tree," Mauriac calls this
poem, and its twelve inevitable lines defy
translation, yet here is an attempt:

The fragrance of your gown lures the bees
More surely than the sandal-crushed fruit.
O greet we this surge of summer's exuberance,
This country quiet in which Pan sleeps!

And dreaming I see you ageless and transfixed,
Feet turned to roots, with arms outstretched,
All your leafy sweet-smelling hair
Tossed wildly by urgent winds.

The wasps will crawl over you
Without alarm to your skin-become-bark,
Where the grasshoppers sing,
And the river-like flow of your blood
Will nourish a world without end.

Reading these lines and remembering
Yu Shan Han's discourse on the Chinese
earth as the matrix of Chinese poetry, I am
convinced that no lasting literature will
come from south of Tehachapi without

marriage between writer and land. And what nuptials could ever fruitfully be consummated on a bed of asphalt, under a kleig-lit, smog-filled sky?

Enough of Hollywood satire and rancho romance of the pre-gringo never-never land! Give us a poet with gimlet eyes, great heart, and sweet voice. If the poet's function is to state a vision, where is the best vantage point for his scrutiny? From a Constellation which takes only fifteen minutes to cross the San Bernardinos and arrow down the valley to the runway? From the rear car of the Chief during its hour-long course along the mountains' ankles from Cajon to city?

Best is the memory of an autumn day, when in a topless roadster of slow speed, festooned with grape leaves, Quince and I and a woodcarving crony, zigzagged a desultory course back to town from a cool morning in a Cucamonga cellar; and at sundown on the crest of Turnbull Canyon craned our necks and saw cameo-clear, cities, plains and people, from Jacinto to Clemente.

Rabelaisian Notes

I MUST CONFESS that my first interest in Rabelais, during college days, was scatological. On the lowest level his work is barnyard-rich in episodes involving the natural functions. There is nothing prurient about it. To satisfy that sophomoric craving we went to *Mademoiselle de Maupin*. The dirt in Rabelais is asexual.

My first knowledge that Rabelais' work exists on other and higher levels came when I was a graduate student in France. An old eagle-beaked Burgundian professor at Dijon, Gaston Roupnel, the author of *Nono*, an earthy novel of the peasantry of the Côte d'Or, was lecturing on Folklore in Rabelais. From auditing these lectures I learned, among other things, of the linguistic debt French literature owes to Rabelais. He is the father of French prose, and gave it an abundant vitality which generations of academicians have not succeeded in gelding. I never mastered Renaissance French any more than I did Chaucerian English, and thus it was not until I encountered the unexpurgated seventeenth-century English translation of Rabelais that I fully realized the sustenance to be had from reading the Frenchman's book in our language.

This translation, commenced by Sir Thomas Urquhart in 1653 and completed by Peter Motteux in 1693, was the first Rabelais in English, and remains the best. It is one of the classics of translation, a treasury of seventeenth-century English. Today's English is not too different from that of 300 years ago, whereas modern French is radically changed from that written by Rabelais in the sixteenth century. Thus modern Frenchmen, unless they are scholars, must read Rabelais in a contemporary version, while Urquhart and Motteux are comprehensible to school children.

I first owned their translation in the one-volume Rarity Press photolith of the Navarre Society's 1922 two-volume edition, illustrated by W. Heath Robinson. Robinson remains my favorite illustrator of Rabelais, second choice being Gustave Doré. The UCLA Library owns a folio set of Rabelais with steel engravings by Doré, to read which one needs a lectern and a derrick.

I have continued to collect Rabelais in cheap editions, until now I own a two- or three-foot shelf of books by and about him. In the libraries which I serve are found more comprehensive collections, from the 1653-1693 translation and revisions of 1708 and 1737, to the definitive French scholarly edition and the so-called American translation of 1929 by Samuel Putnam.

For the Limited Editions Club a new English translation was made by Jacques LeClerc. This is the version used in the Modern Library Giant edition. An English don named W. F. Smith translated Rabelais in the nineties. Putnam, LeClerc, and Smith are more literally faithful to Rabelais than are Urquhart-Motteux, just as modern versions of the Bible are more scholarly than the King James. Whereas Rabelais' original text contained 130,000 words, the seventeenth-century translation expanded it to 200,000—and the result was an English masterpiece.

It is in the World's Classics that we find one of the most satisfying of all editions. The price is low, the size handy, the type and printing excellent, the text is unexpurgated Urquhart-Motteux, and the anonymous introduction and notes provide a helpful guide to the land of Rabelais.

This World's Classics edition first appeared in 1934. Three years earlier Harcourt, Brace published an edition of the Urquhart-Motteux version, newly introduced and annotated by Albert Jay Nock and Catherine Wilson. This is the most scholarly of all English editions, illustrated from original documents and engravings; the two sturdy quarto volumes, beautifully designed by Robert Josephy, were issued at $15.00. I bought my set in 1937 at a remainder price of $4.00.

Nock's introduction occupies 196 pages and was also issued separately by Harper. It is the best of all the writings about Rabelais, at the same time learned and simple, razor-edged and tolerant. In 1934 Nock published a 300-page, topographical footnote to his edition of Rabelais, entitled *A Journey Into Rabelais's France*. After reading this too short book I wrote an appreciative letter to Mr. Nock, which brought a friendly reply from him at the Players in New York. Later I sent him a copy of Perry Stricker's *Fragment in the Manner of Rabelais*, and again he wrote me a letter which I cherish. Nock is the closest America has come to producing a Norman Douglas.

It is my hope to return to France someday and follow Nock over Rabelais' trail, from his birthplace near Chinon in Touraine, to Poitiers and Paris, thence to Montpellier where he became a Doctor of Physick and Lyon where he was a resident hospital surgeon, to the Isles of Hyères and Rome, to Metz, place of exile, and finally to Paris where he was buried in 1553.

All the richness of Renaissance Europe is preserved in his book. Learning, skepticism, earthy vitality, and narrative power immortalize the work of this friar turned doctor into writer. He was a great, good man in his own age, protected by Francis the First, physician to cardinals, the peer of Erasmus. In his masterpiece of Gargantua and Pantagruel he created a work which will continue to live on its various levels—animalistic, linguistic, and philosophic—as long as men read books and seek the shadow of a great rock in a weary land.

"My adorable old Rabelais," exclaimed Barbey d'Aurevilly a century ago, "a mastodon radiantly emerged from the blue of a nascent world." Verily!

Chevalier de Seingalt

EVER SINCE Casanova's Memoirs first appeared in print, nearly a century ago, they have been recognized as a masterpiece of autobiography. Their first success came in fact before the ink on the manuscript was entirely dry and they were being circulated among the author's friends. "Send me quickly," wrote the Prince de Ligne to the aged Casanova, "the third volume of your Memoirs. The Count of Salmour, who sends you a thousand greetings, has devoured them and hungers for more."

Today Casanova is one of the three or four most widely printed and read authors of the eighteenth century, in spite of the fact that he has been snubbed by Hutchins' Hundred. Nor has he lacked readers in high places. John Fiske's copy of the Memoirs was well worn. Mark Twain's is annotated. Justice Holmes, it is said, turned to the Venetian for relaxation if not instruction.

Casanova has become a byword for erotica, just as Rabelais stands in the popular mind as a symbol of grossness. It is true that Casanova is erotic and Rabelais gross, but the works of these two men are much more than popular opinion credits them with being.

Casanova's Memoirs actually form an encyclopedia of Europe in the eighteenth century. His life covered three-quarters of the century, he traveled everywhere, knew everyone, did everything; and when he was sixty years old settled down as—of all things — librarian to a Bohemian count. Then to relieve the boredom of his final dozen years Casanova employed his prodigious memory and fluent pen to write the story of the first forty-seven years of his life. To corrupt Shaw's epigram on teachers, as long as Casanova could, he did; and when he arrived at the age when he couldn't, he wrote.

The result is generally conceded to be the greatest autobiography ever written. More human than St. Augustine, more truthful than Cellini, more complex and dramatic than Pepys, less prosaic than Evelyn, more objective than Rousseau, Casanova's Memoirs furnish not only the myriad details of his dynamic life, but also a masterful description of the century in which he lived, the habits of chambermaids and queens, coachmen and kings, the conversations of poets and philosophers, and the personal appearance of almost every person of international renown.

It is thanks to Casanova most of all that we know so much of the daily life of the eighteenth century; of its theaters, cafés, balls, festivals, inns, brothels, stage-coaches, castles, monasteries, and nunneries. From Casanova we learn how Europe traveled, gambled, ate, loved, fought, and died. His Memoirs have outlived all the newspapers and most of the books of the century; they have the eternal freshness of a mirror.

From the midpoint of our century of universal death and destruction how nostalgic seems the eighteenth, the Century of Reason! "He who has not lived in the years near to 1789," said Talleyrand, "does not know how sweet life can be." The century was sweet and pleasant—to those who had the wealth and leisure to enjoy it. A common culture had reached high noon. There were no widespread or prolonged wars or violent political upheavals between the Bloodless Revolution of 1688 in England and the French Revolution of 1789. The fruits of the Renaissance hung ripe in the orchards of western Europe. The music of Bach, Handel, and Mozart made the century supreme in this form of art. It was perhaps the West's last sweet lull before the storms which, ever since Napoleon and the Industrial Revolution, have blown with increasing violence.

The picture which Casanova paints of

the eighteenth century is neither abstract nor romanticized; it is more like a Breughel. His canvas swarms with people in action, not with ideas. As Stefan Zweig wrote, "It is the best-stocked menagerie of human beings that any one writer has ever packed into the enclosure of a single book."

And this is the reason why the Memoirs are one of the world's immortal books. They teem with life. The erotic element is not such a large part, when you come to analyze the Memoirs. In the ordinary erotic book the reader skips over the passages which link the amatory business. Nothing about Casanova is ordinary. We find ourselves devouring every word, no matter what the subject, and wishing there were twice as many. For Casanova savored life down to its last detail, and had the power as a writer to infuse the reader with his enormous gusto.

There are even those who find Casanova's love affairs the dullest part of his book, and skip over them to what they regard as the real meat of the Memoirs—his intellectual encounters with Voltaire, d'Alembert and Crébillon, his descriptions of city and court life, his duels and escapes from prison. In fact, the famous escape from the Leads—the Venetian State Prison —is probably the best-known episode in all the four thousand pages of the Memoirs. And it is one of the most thrilling adventure stories ever written. Subsequent research in the Venetian archives has revealed Casanova to have told the truth about this escape; a ledger was found wherein was listed the cost of repairs to the damage done by him in making his getaway.

It was no accident that Casanova wrote well. All his life he had wielded an active pen and had written works on mathematics, history, philology, government, finance, astronomy and gastronomy. He was a tireless letter-writer, and his correspondence has been unearthed from a dozen places over the Continent. The physical and intellectual experience of his first sixty years was the perfect preparation for the writing of an autobiography; and he put into its composition days and months and years of work at his desk, even getting up in the middle of the night to unburden his teeming brain on paper.

I know of no study of Casanova as a writer, of his vocabulary and style, of the way he obtains his effects. Take his dialogue, for example; he is master of this most difficult of techniques, in knowing how to use conversation as it should be used, to advance narrative and to reveal character. The strength of the Memoirs comes from their solid construction on specific event and concrete detail.

It was Somerset Maugham, I believe,

who advised young writers seeking to extend their vocabulary to copy verbatim the whole of the Urquhart-Motteux translation of Rabelais. Likewise would I recommend a study of Casanova to writers who would master the art of narration and of dialogue.

Who was Giacomo Giralamo Casanova, self-styled Chevalier de Seingalt? Born a Venetian, the eldest of six children of a dancing master and a third-rate actress, he studied first for the church, then for law at Padua, later became a soldier, and finally settled down in earnest as an adventurer and gambler, to pry open the plump European oyster.

Casanova was no ordinary rogue. He had an encylopedic, though superficial, mind. Venice knew him as an abbé, a violinist and a wit; in Paris he operated as a manufacturer, financier and economist; in Holland he was an alchemist and astronomer. Other towns in Europe saw him in the guise of a historian, a sorcerer and mathematician; Catherine the Great heard with pleasure his discourse on the calendar; in Poland and Russia he inspected mines, in Spain he nearly became the governor of an agricultural colony.

To his contemporararies Casanova was not known as a gross sensualist, and if he had not written his Memoirs, the names of most of his loves would not be known; and

he would survive today, if at all, in foot-
notes as merely a roving adventurer of
unusual intellectual interests. His contemporary reputations were several. The
police archives of Paris and Vienna, for
example, reveal him as a rogue, an impos-
tor, a forger and jailbird, whereas the
Prince de Ligne in his memoirs laments
the many interesting characters he has
known and lost, and lists Casanova among
Louis XV, Frederick the Great, Potemkin
and others. Elsewhere the Prince says, "I
have lived with Beaumarchais, Crébillon,
d'Alembert, Hume and Casanova."

Where did Casanova get the title "Chevalier de Seingalt"? When the Mayor of
Augsburg asked him this question, Casanova replied that the alphabet was common property, and that like Voltaire he
had taken eight letters from it and arranged them to form his second name;
since no one else, to his knowledge, pos-
sessed this name, it could not be robbery.
The Mayor was hardly satisfied with this
explanation, but he was forced to agree
with Casanova's argument that he was following the example of posterity, otherwise
everyone would still bear the name of
Adam.

An interesting account of Casanova as
bibliophile could be compiled from the
Memoirs. I have already noted that he
ended his days as a librarian, to the Count

Waldstein of Dux in Bohemia. Although this was essentially a sinecure, Casanova did devote himself to the keeping of the 25,000 volumes. For at least a century after his death the library remained just as he arranged it (every librarian's dream!), and was described by Arthur Symons after his visit to Dux in 1899. Symons discovered there a cache of Casanova's manuscripts, letters and papers, including two missing chapters of the Memoirs.

Casanova paid at least two tributes to libraries which he used in the course of his wanderings. One is to a Jesuit library in Rome, to which he was given special access. "Two or three weeks after my arrival," he writes, "the Prince of Santa Croce heard me complaining of the obstacles to research in Roman libraries, and he offered to give me an introduction to the Superior of the Jesuits. I accepted the offer, and was made free of the library; I could not only go and read when I liked, but I could, on writing my name down, take books away with me. The keepers of the library always brought me candles when it grew dark, and their politeness was so great that they gave me the key of a side door, so that I could slip in and out as I pleased."

At Wolfenbüttel in Germany, while recuperating from illness, Casanova worked in what he described as the third largest

library in Europe. "The learned librarian," he writes, "whose politeness was all
the better for being completely devoid of
affectation, told me that not only could I
have whatever books I wished to see, but
that I could take them to my lodging, not
even excepting the manuscripts, which are
the chief feature in that fine library. I
spent a week in the library, only leaving
it to take my meals and go to bed, and I
count this week as one of the happiest I
have ever spent, for then I forgot myself
completely; and in the delight of study,
the past, the present, and the future were
entirely blotted out. Of some such sort, I
think, must be the joys of the redeemed."

What was the basis of Casanova's extraordinary success with women? His physical endowment was part of it, the Prince
de Ligne describing him as "built like Her-
cules"; but more important was his profound understanding of feminine psy-
chology. There were no secrets or tricks
involved, nor did he ape Ovid in compiling
a treatise on the art of love. Casanova's
success was due in great measure to his
mastery of what Havelock Ellis calls the
secondary law of courting, namely, the
development in the male of an imaginative attentiveness to the physical and bod-
ily states of the female, in place of an
exclusive attentiveness to his own gratifi-
cation. He sought his pleasure in the pleas-

ure, and not in the complaisance, of the women he loved, and they recognized gratefully his skill.

The Memoirs have a confusing bibliographical history. Written in French by an Italian, they were first published in a German translation a quarter-century after the author's death. A French translation, pirated from the German, led the firm of Brockhaus (to which the original manuscript had been sold by the nephew into whose hands it passed upon Casanova's death) to publish the original French version. But not until after it had been somewhat edited for style and content by Jules Laforgue, a French professor of Dresden.

Casanova's Memoirs have yet to be published exactly as they were written. For over a century Brockhaus has zealously guarded the manuscript in its vault. I have yet to learn the fate of this publisher's archives in the British bombing raids on Leipzig.

The first partial English translation in book form appeared at Brunswick, in 1863, in six incomplete volumes. This set is of great rarity. Thirty years passed then before the Laforgue French edition was translated by Arthur Machen. This work was reprinted later, with the addition of the missing chapters discovered by Arthur Symons at Dux. The Italians published a fourteen-volume edition at Rome, from

1882 to 1888. The Germans issued a scholarly edition in fifteen volumes, from 1907 to 1913, but the most nearly definitive edition thus far to appear is that published in French in twelve volumes, commencing in 1924. The notes to this La Sirène edition incorporate the minute historical findings of an international band of Casanova scholars—German, Austrian, Danish, Italian, French and English—who have devoted immense labors to the attempted verification and explanation of every detail in the Memoirs.

The result has been to substantiate the essential truth of Casanova's autobiography. Writing years after the events which he was describing took place, it is natural that his dates and chronological sequences are often faulty. And he lies shamelessly about his motivations in certain instances. He leaves out many of his misadventures with the police authorities, and the Memoirs close before he came to the period in his fifties when he served as a police spy in Venice.

It was not until 1940 that an annotated English version of the Memoirs was published. The Limited Editions Club commissioned Arthur Machen to translate the notes to the La Sirène edition, and appended them to his translation of the text made half a century earlier. The Machen translation is a masterpiece of this difficult art, and to his version of the French notes the aged Welshman added sage and pungent comment of his own, which makes them almost as good reading as the text.

It would require a separate book to review the books and studies on Casanova. We have items on his adventures in England, in Paris, in Switzerland in general and Geneva in particular, in Bologna, in Rome and in Cologne. A Casanova Society was formed in France twenty years ago, devoted to the publication of his works other than the Memoirs; eight volumes have thus far appeared. Of the relatively few books in English on Casanova the best is by the American, Guy Endore, called *Casanova, His Known and Unknown Life*, which appeared in 1929. As for the vast number of novels, stories and poems mined by writers from the treasure of the Memoirs, these range from Thackeray to Schnitzler to Richard Aldington.

Of all that I have read about Casanova my favorite piece is by Stefan Zweig in his *Adepts in Self Portraiture*, and I shall borrow his peroration for my own:

"The most skilful psychologist, the most practised writer, cannot make of Casanova a more live figure than he makes of himself in virtue of his absolute, unreflecting nonchalance. He stands before our eyes in all sorts of situations. We see him in anger, when his face flushes, when his white teeth are clenched, when his mouth is bitter as gall; we see him in danger, bold, alert, smiling contemptuously, with a steady hand on the hilt of his sword. We see him in good society; vain, boastful, self-possessed, talking easily, voluptuously appraising the charms of women. Whether as a handsome stripling or as a toothless ruin, he is always vividly presented to us. When we read his memoirs, we feel as if he were actually before us; and we are sure that if this man, dead long since, were to come suddenly round the corner, we should recognize him in a moment — though we know him only through a self-portrait limned by one who was neither a professional author nor a psychologist.

"It is of no use, therefore, to turn up your nose at his equivocal talent, or to put on moral airs because of his scapegrace behavior, or to hold him to account for his banalities and ignorant plagiarisms in matters philosophical. Despite all you can do, despite all the objections you can raise, Giacomo Casanova has taken his place in world literature, beside the gallows-bird Villon, and various other rogues, who will outlive countless thoroughly reputable authors and critics. As when he was alive, so after his death, he has reduced to absurdity all the accepted laws of aesthetics, and has thrown the moral catechism into the waste-paper basket. The growth and the

persistence of his reputation show that a
man need not be especially gifted, industrious, well-behaved, noble-minded, and
sublime, in order to make his way into the
temple of literary immortality. Casanova
has proved that one may write the most
amusing story in the world without being
a novelist, and may give the most admi-
rable picture of the time without being a
historian; for in the last resort we judge
these matters not by the method but by
the effect, not by the morality but by the
power. Any thoroughly adequate feeling
may be productive, shamelessness just as
much as shame, characterlessness just as
much as character, evil just as much as
good, morality just as much as immorality.
What decides whether a man will become
immortal, is not his character but his vitality. Nothing save intensity confers immortality. A man manifests himself more
vividly, in proportion as he is strong and
unified, effective and unique. Immortality
knows nothing of morality or immorality,
of good or evil; it measures only work and
strength; it demands from a man not pur-
ity but unity. Here, morality is nothing;
intensity, all."

The Enjoyment of Joyce

I KNEW THE moment I saw it that it was a book for me. Bound in finely woven gray buckram stamped in red, printed in Baskerville on 792 pages of India paper, it was a compact volume, measuring six by four inches, three-quarters of an inch thick. I paid 39.50 lire ($2) to the bookseller and thrust the volume in my pocket without another look. Ever since boyhood I have liked to carry a keenly desired book home from shop or library, to where it could first be gloated over, then savored without interruption.

Fortunate the reader who encounters a long-sought book at the inevitable time and place in his life, for then the reading of it under perfectly conjoined conditions is unforgettable. Such was my experience with the Odyssey Press edition of *Ulysses*, in the fair city of Florence, one rainy winter a decade after its first monumental quarto printing, by Darantière of Dijon, in the year 1922.

I had a room on the top floor of a *pensione* in one of the old palaces on the Lungarno Guicciardini, one window of which overlooked the Arno and another offered a view of a rough sea of rosy-tiled roofs. It was a cozy room, warmed by a pot-bellied stove called a *porcellino*. Breakfast was brought up, together with a basket of pine faggots, and while the pluvial mornings dripped and gurgled away, I sat by the river window, reading Joyce's masterpiece and looking up now and then for a sight of the coffee-colored water flowing high under the lovely arch of Ponte Santa Trinità. In a nearby room a fellow boarder was practicing Bach sonatas for unaccompanied violin. I read only a few pages each morning, before wading forth to the American Express for those quintessential letters from Quince, thence to a cafe for a *piccola birra*, a glance at the paper and the passing ankles, followed by lunch at the *pensione*, and afternoons in the libraries and galleries.

By dint of unusual self-control I rationed the 792 pages, so that the book lasted me three months. It was the perfect regime for reading a masterpiece. No telephone, no friends, no car—nothing but myself sheltered and fed, in a beautiful city, with a life-stuffed book about one man's day in Dublin. It took Joyce seven years to write *Ulysses*, working successively in Trieste, Zürich, and Paris. I made the reading of it last me twelve weeks, and shed a tear the day I finally came to the last ardent words of Molly Bloom's nocturnal soliloquy.

The book was so much greater than I had been led to believe from all the noisy notoriety the censors had gained for it. There it was, a huge roadblock at the end of the long line of the English novel; a novel to end novels, or so it seemed to me at the time; and it was only the blind ambition of youth which led me to continue work on my attempt at the "great American novel."

In it Joyce displayed an absolute mastery of English prose, ranging from the simplest Biblical narration and a *tour de force* recapitulation of centuries of English style, to a stream-of-consciousness conclusion which has had an enormous influence on novelists writing since 1922. I care not a fig for those who find *Ulysses* too long or too involved or too . . . It needs no réclame by me. It is.

Since that introduction to Joyce I have read most of his other work and have assembled a small collection of books by and about him. For those who want to explore Joyce the best sampling of his prose is *Introducing James Joyce*, a selection by T. S. Eliot, published by Faber and Faber as one of their Sesame Books. A good study of the man and his work is by Harry Levin, in New Directions' Makers of Modern Literature series, while the same editor's *The Portable Joyce* ranges from the simple stories of Dubliners to the bewildering apotheosis of *Finnegan's Wake*. Paul Jordan-Smith's *A Key to the Ulysses of James Joyce* (1927) is still helpful in tracing the peregrinations of Leopold Bloom.

Next to the Odyssey Press *Ulysses* my favorite piece of Joyce is *Pomes Penyeach*, a tiny book published at Paris in 1927 by Shakespeare & Co. My copy has association interest in that it was a gift to me from the publisher, Sylvia Beach. Typical of the lyric beauty of Joyce's verse is the poem:

BAHNHOFSTRASSE

The eyes that mock me sign the way
Whereto I pass at eve of day,

Grey way whose violet signals are
The trysting and the twining star.

Ah star of evil! Star of pain!
Highhearted youth comes not again

Nor old heart's wisdom yet to know
The signs that mock me as I go.

Lines on Lawrence

OFF AND ON for twenty years I have been reading and collecting D. H. Lawrence. It started during my last year in college when a friend gave me a copy of *Sons & Lovers* in the Modern Library edition. I still have it, the cornerstone on which I built one of the few author collections that has never failed to yield me pleasure. In 1934 I was planning a biographical and critical study of Lawrence, and I annotated my copies of his book. They are for the most part inexpensive later printings; the value of the collection being its virtual completeness — everything written by Lawrence and nearly every book and pamphlet written about him, in half a dozen languages including the Japanese. In 1937 I cataloged Lawrence's manuscripts and a few years later made an annotated list of the books about Lawrence; both works were printed by Ward Ritchie.

I never met Lawrence or corresponded with him, but I have had the great experience of knowing his widow Frieda, of talking with many of his friends, and of visiting his graves, at Vence on the French

Riviera, and later to where his remains were removed, on his New Mexican ranch near Taos.

My own reading and collecting interests are broad and varied, and in Lawrence I have found a satisfying author who wrote much on many subjects, employing various forms of literature and ranging the world for the settings of his books. He was novelist, storyist, poet, essayist, dramatist, travelist, and ever and always a supreme epistolographer.

The thick volume of his Letters, edited by his friend Aldous Huxley, reached me in Dijon soon after it was published in the autumn of 1932, two and a half years after Lawrence's death at 45. My thesis on Robinson Jeffers was being printed then at the press of Bernigaud & Privat, in the Rue Berbisey, to which I went every afternoon to return corrected galley proofs (the monotypist knew no English and I was kept busy!) and to pick up a newly set batch. My favorite reading haunt at the time was the tiny Café du Raisin in the Rue Monge, in the apartment above which the great tragic poet Crébillon had been born in 1674; and there at a corner table, with a glass of vin blanc-cassis (Dijon's favorite apéritif) at my elbow, I made preliminary corrections on the proofs. That done, I dug Lawrence's Letters from my book bag, and for an hour before dinner, while the cafe grew noisier and noisier with the hoarse Burgundian *patois* of the workers, I savored those letters in the same deliberate way in which I was to read *Ulysses* a year later.

The volume of Letters has traveled with me since then to many strange places, but the little cafe setting, where I first read what are surely among the best letters ever written, is always the first image which comes to memory when I open the book or even see it on my shelf.

Every one of my Lawrence books has this evocative power in varying degree. The beautiful Black Sun edition of *The Escaped Cock* was the first book I bought in Paris, and the mere sight of it recalls my first olfactory impression of that river city —a bittersweet blend of coal smoke and Chancl. *The Plumed Serpent* I first read in Rome, in a *pensione* near the top of the Spanish Steps, to the music of the Clock Symphony — incongruous combination! We read *The Rainbow* aloud on our honeymoon, on the sea-cliff south of Laguna. My copy of his finest travel book, *Sea and Sardinia*, was pearled from the cavern of Holmes Book Store in Los Angeles. In his Australian novel, *Kangaroo*, the chapter called "The Nightmare" describes his wartime ordeal in England, and how he gleaned the golden chips left by the woodchoppers; mere sight of the book fills my nostrils with the faintly sweet smell of freshly chopped oak wood.

And here is a brown cloth-bound volume whose title-page reads: *Movements in European History*, by Lawrence H. Davidson, Oxford University Press, 1921; and on the flyleaf, in a child's careful hand, is written "Vera Brereton, Middle 5th." It is one of the scarcest, least-known items in all the Lawrence canon: a school text written by him from the depths of the débacle following suppression of *The Rainbow*, when his name was held in such opprobrium as to cause his scholarly publisher, Humphry Milford, to insist on a pseudonym. By 1925 the cloud had passed, and Oxford issued an illustrated edition under Lawrence's own name. The text was used for years in the Irish schools and may still be, for all I know.

Ward Ritchie ferreted out this copy in London for ten shillings, and mailed it across the channel to me. Inserted is a letter to me from Frieda Lawrence, recalling the circumstances under which the book was written. She recalls that for the Irish edition Lawrence was asked to change "Pope's mistress" to "Pope's friend." I have gone through the book, marking Lawrentian passages, from which even a superficial student of his style could recognize his authorship.

And here is my copy of Lawrence's first

book, *The White Peacock*, and it is far removed from the valuable first edition of
1910—an Albatross reprint which I had
bound in Nice, the binder's stamp tells me,
for a cost of 48 cents. I remember the day
I called for it at the bindery, put it in my
pocket — a sandwich in the other — and
took the bus to Villefranche. Up a steep
path I trudged, and when I was high above
the colored stucco houses I scaled a slip-
pery rock-face, with my shoes tied together
and slung around my neck, until I reached
an eyrie. There under a pollen-dropping
pine I lay at ease, read Lawrence, ate
sandwich, peered down at the pastel town
and the postcard-blue bay, and meditated
on the peoples who had come before me—
Phoenician, Greek, Roman, Goth, wave
upon wave of the voracious generations,
and I, hungry as any other, and as fugitive.

The wonderful quality about *The White
Peacock* and Lawrence's other early novels, *Sons & Lovers* and *The Rainbow*, is
their evocation of the English countryside,
in a prose at once poetical and exact. I
remember when I first read them, how
barren in contrast seemed the countryside
of my own southern California, devoid of
seasonal vegetation, ancient farms and
manors, churches and bridges. In those
days of desire to be a novelist, my fancy
fastened on such local landmarks as the
Old Mill and the Raymond Hotel, and

peopled them with an imaginary peasantry.

It was these English books of Lawrence
which, paradoxically, revealed my home-
land to me. The heavily wooded Bilicke
Hill on Monterey Road, with its great vine-
covered house, also had possibilities as a
romantic setting; and one of my favorite
reveries while far from home was of making a fortune and returning to South Pasadena to buy the Bilicke estate and set myself up thereon as lord of the manor! Not
long ago I drove along Monterey Road and
saw a For Sale sign on the property. I hur-
ried by, with no regret for the lost dream.
Subdivision, overpopulation, industrial-
ization, mechanized madness under a pall
of smog: what successful ruin we have
wrought!

And thus it is for various reasons that
my Lawrence collection remains for me a
lively lot of books, not the least of which
is that they have heightened and widened
my own awareness and responsiveness to
life—a good measuring stick for any work
of art.

Lady Chatterley's Lover

MY OWN JUDGMENT of his last novel is the same now as when I first read it twenty years ago. It was an estimate based on a reading of the book itself, not upon what others said about it. Since it was first published in 1928 *Lady Chatterley's Lover* has attained world-wide notoriety. I sensed it then and I know it now to be one of the most vital novels ever written; significant because it drove a new road into the mysterious heartland of man's sexual life. This it did by describing in language both tender and coarse the prelude, the consummation, and the afterglow of sexual intercourse. To the love-act Lawrence brought two unsatisfied people who had been deeply wounded by life, and through it gave them fulfilment and healing.

During these two decades since I first read *Lady Chatterley* I have heard it discussed by many people in several countries. Opinion is usually violently for or against. It has been castigated for its social philosophy and technical faults, as well as for its intimate subject matter and frank language. In a French salon I heard a countess chastise Lawrence not for the lovemaking, but for where the love was made! Only the lower animals, she declared, make love out of doors.

I never bothered to champion *Lady Chatterley*. I liked it on first reading and I like it now, after many rereadings, because it is pure Lawrence in vision, detail, and execution. Although fussy analysis reveals faults of detail, the total effect is faultless. It was written from Lawrence's mature and passionate belief that man's and mankind's ills, both psychic and economic, can be cured by the practice of what he calls phallic tenderness. Thus Lawrence smote Philistines and Freudians, Fabians and Bolsheviks with one erotic thunderbolt.

This was a new road for him; his earlier novels, especially *The Rainbow*, *Women in Love*, and *The Plumed Serpent*, were battle-reports on the war between men and women. In *Lady Chatterley* and its companion novella *The Escaped Cock* (known also as *The Man Who Died*) he brought peace through personal orgasm rather than by social intercourse.

Most people believe that because of its intimate nature sexual congress should be above (or below) literary description. Lawrence used our ancient four-letter words to flout the taboo. He seized the English novel by the scruff of the neck and

booted it from bedroom to barnyard. And
it is the outdoor setting of the novel that is
to me one of its great delights. For its locale
Lawrence returned to his native Midlands,
the scene of his earliest novels beginning
with *The White Peacock*; and his descriptions of the woods in spring, flower-bright
or rain-gray, are sheer prose poetry.

Lawrence wrote *Lady Chatterley* in
Tuscany just two years before his death,
and in it embodied his mature judgment
of life. It took faith to write it and courage
to publish it. Official England greeted it
with vituperation. No Anglo-American
publisher has ever dared openly to issue
the book, and it was only after Lawrence's
death that an expurgated version appeared. It has been pirated many times. Of
three separate manuscript versions, Lawrence published the last. The first draft
appeared recently in expurgated form as
The First Lady Chatterley.

I have no doubt that *Lady Chatterley* is
destined for literary immortality, for in
theme and treatment it is as unique as
Ulysses. It has not been my practice in
these essays to use authorities to prop my
prejudices. And yet why deny my delight
when I find myself in company with such
masters as Yeats and Shaw in praising
Lady C.?

Yeats did not read Lawrence's book until
1933, three years after the author's death,

and then he wrote about it in a letter to a friend:

"My two sensations at the moment are Hulme's *Speculations* and *Lady Chatterley's Lover* . . . Frank Harris's Memoirs were vulgar and unmoral — the sexual patches were like holes burned with a match in a piece of old newspaper. Their appeal to physical sensation was hateful but Lady Chatterley is noble. The description of the sexual act is more detailed than in Harris, the language is sometimes that of a cabman and yet the book is all fire. Those two lovers, the gamekeeper and his employer's wife, each separated from their class by their love and by fate are poignant in their loneliness; the coarse language of the one accepted by both becomes a forlorn poetry, uniting their solitudes, something ancient, humble and terrible."

Shaw's reaction was typically Shavian in that he prescribed a pedagogical use for the book.

"If I had a marriageable daughter," he asked, "what could I give her to prepare her? Dickens? Thackeray? George Eliot? Walter Scott? Trollope? Or even any of the clever modern women who take such a fiendish delight in writing very able novels that leave you hopeless and miserable? They would teach her a lot about life and society and human nature. But they would leave her absolutely in the dark as to mar-

riage. Even Fielding and Joyce and George
Moore would be no use: instead of telling
her nothing they would tell her worse
than nothing. But she would learn something from *Lady Chatterley*. I shouldn't
let her engage herself if I could help it
until she had read that book. Lawrence
had delicacy enough to tell the best, and
brutality enough to rub in the worst. *Lady
Chatterley* should be on the shelves of
every college for budding girls. They
should be forced to read it on pain of being
refused a marriage license."

Surely not a bad idea, to make this novel
a *vade mecum* for beginners! In this age of
pornographic movies and magazines and
billboard debauchery, how simple and
pure seems Lawrence's vision.

The *editio princeps* was privately
printed at Florence in 1928 by L. Fran-
ceschini in a handsome octavo, limited to
a thousand copies numbered and signed by
Lawrence. The paper is a creamy deckle-
edged rag, the binding a mulberry paper
over boards, labeled on the spine, and
wrapped in an unprinted cream-colored
jacket. My copy is Number 52, and I acquired it only recently from a cache of
copies unearthed after the death of the
book's publisher, Orioli. Also from his estate came my copy of the rarest of all editions of the novel—the second, of which
only 200 copies were published, also in

1928 by Orioli in Florence, from the same type, but on cheap paper and in mulberry wrappers. It was only through references in Lawrence's letters to Orioli that I knew of this elusive second edition, and for years I failed to find a copy or even a Lawrence collector who owned or had ever seen or heard of one. Because of its cheap format and avid readers it is certain that most of this edition was rapidly destroyed.

I have also two other authorized editions, one issued by Lawrence at Paris in 1929 in cheap format to undersell the pirates and containing his foreword "My Skirmish with the Jolly Roger." The other is the posthumous Odyssey Press edition, sponsored by Lawrence's widow Frieda in 1933, with a preface written, she told me, by the publisher for her to sign. It is a nicely printed book, similar in format to the same press's *Ulysses*, and I bought it likewise in Florence and had it bound there in characteristic Italian floral paper over boards.

If I had no other books at all, I would feel rich enough as long as *Lady Chatterley* was mine to have and to hold.

Glory of Life

ONCE UPON a time when I was a starveling book clerk there arrived in the shop a book of rare beauty in form and content, a three-guinea book, ordered especially from England for a collector of fine printing. I smuggled it home overnight, and by dint of desperate typing I made a copy of the nine-thousand word essay for my own leisurely reading. The book was the Golden Cockerel Press edition of *Glory of Life*, an essay in epicureanism by Llewelyn Powys, and a glorious piece of bookmaking, with title printed in red, and wood-engraved illustrations by Robert Gibbings. Someday, I vowed, when my ship came in, I would trade my typescript for one of the 277 printed copies of that credo which I took (and still do) for my own.

Fifteen years have passed, and of all the material things they have brought me I cherish none more than the copy of *Glory of Life* which I acquired two years ago from a bookseller in Guildford. I have also a copy of the John Lane edition of this essay, a thin octavo whose frontispiece is an Emery Walker reproduction of Breughel's

"The Harvesters." At six shillings a copy I gladly bought several to give away to friends. Until American publishers produce books of such merit at modest prices, I shall continue to export most of my book dollars to Britain.

And now I must confess that when I was in college, John Cowper Powys was the only one of that amazing literary family who held my interest. I devoured his two-volume novel *Wolf Solent*, a page of which now would give me indigestion. Gregg Anderson had better taste. In 1928 he reprinted from the *Atlantic Monthly* twenty-five copies of Llewelyn Powys' history-haunted essay "Out of the Past." Gregg's own copy was given to me by his widow, Caroline, with an inserted autograph letter from Powys. Never have I relished the work of T. F. Powys, whose lean stories afford me no nourishment. Slight but charming is Philippa Powys' gypsy novel, *The Blackthorn Winter*, while Architect A. R. Powys' *The Repair of Ancient Buildings* led me to search out those four delightful books on the old bridges of Britain, written on behalf of the Society for the Protection of Ancient Buildings.

I came late to Llewelyn's work, although during the 1920's his books appeared frequently in the United States, and before they did in England. Harcourt, Brace published several autobiographical and travel books—*Ebony and Ivory*, *Black Laughter*, *Skin for Skin*, *The Verdict of Bridlegoose* —which have long been out of print. In the 1930's both countries issued occasional books by him, of which *A Pagan's Pilgrimage* (to the Holy Land) and *Now That the Gods Are Dead*, are the ones I like best. In 1941 his posthumous novel, *Love and Death*, had difficulty in finding an American publisher, before Simon & Schuster would risk it. English publication only was obtained for a subsequent volume of letters, one of Swiss essays, and a biography by Malcolm Elwin.

Llewelyn Powys is not expensive to collect. The Golden Cockerel *Glory* and that press's later *Book of Days* are probably the dearest of all his thirty-odd titles, and not as Powys items but because they are fine-press books. No, his books are not expensive—when they can be found; for as all collectors know, some books are almost impossible to find, for the very reason that there is no demand for them. Two titles he wrote in 1924 for the Haldeman-Julius Little Blue Books—*Honey and Gall* and *Cup-Bearers of Wine and Hellebore* —can be had for a nickel or a dime, if one knows where to look. Perhaps they are still in print.

My reading and collecting of Llewelyn Powys has been casual and intermittent. At different times in my life his books have appeared on my shelves, partly by chance, and yet somehow in answer to an inner need for the content of that particular book. My reading has always been extremely personal—why deny it?—a hungry search for books to feed my own prejudices, as well as to strengthen my weaknesses, an earnest quest for verification of my own experience.

And it is here that Llewelyn Powys has never failed me. I find in him so many points of identity: travel to the same places, a sense of history, love of the tangible here-and-now rather than a vague hereafter, a passion for seasonal earth, a devotion to such masters as Montaigne, Burton and Rabelais, and a fondness for written English of the seventeenth century.

When I happened on his first novel, *Apples Be Ripe*, on the bargain table at Dawson's, that simple tale of rural England reached me as a life preserver; for at the time I read it I was at a crisis in my own life. Although I made an opposite decision from Powys' protagonist, who quit school-teaching to become a gypsy, I was strengthened in my resolution to devote my life to Bibliotheca rather than Bohemia, by the vicarious fulfilment I derived from reading this novel.

> Apples be ripe, nuts be brown,
> Petticoats up and trousers down.

runs the old couplet which served Powys for title, and it gives one more than a vague idea of the book's philosophy.

One evening at our house, when Richard Aldington picked up *Apples Be Ripe* and glanced through it, then stopped to read a passage, I lamented how quickly it had gone out of print, after selling fewer than five thousand copies. Whereupon the author of *All Men Are Enemies*, an equally pagan book, remarked how little the average reader appreciates the devoted toil that goes into the creation of such apparently simple books, and how quickly they become lost amid the litter of jackpot literature. True, I said, but the current cheapies do rot away, leaving gem-like books, such as *Apples Be Ripe*, to shine forth for the discerning to see.

Llewelyn Powys' only other novel is *Love and Death*, a prose poem to shelve alongside *Love in the Valley* and *Daphnis and Chloe*. Sooner or later it will come back into print; and not have to wait as long, I hope, as George Thornley's 1657 edition of Longus, which barely survived in three or four copies, until Ricketts and Shannon discovered and reprinted it at their Vale Press in 1893, the first and best of the numerous reprints of this translation of what has been called the first novel.

Llewelyn Powys' essays are among the best I have ever read. Mellow in philosophy, precise in observation of nature, couched in a rich yet supple English, they are to be found in such volumes as *Earth Memories*, *Dorset Essays*, *Somerset Essays*, and *Swiss Essays*. His *Letters*, edited by Louis Wilkinson, with an introduction by his widow, Alyse Gregory, is a wartime selection of only half of the extant epistles. He was a great letter writer, tolerant, wise and humorous, at the same time impassioned and commonsensical. Up to the very end of his life (he died in Switzerland on December 2, 1939) his spirit was unquenched. On November 19th he wrote characteristically to his brother Willie:

"What a wonder if I really get better again! It will be just by cunning and patience, or God's will, or Lulu's luck, but once on my feet I will creep about quietlike, on fox feet so I can still wag my ears above ground with fox-glove flowers. There was once an old man who was carrying a load home to his cottage, a heavy bloody load of great buggerly brands. Tired of the crusts he ate, of being ill clothed, ill fed and over-worked, he threw the load on the ground and called upon Death to come. In a moment Death was at his elbow and asked 'What do 'ee lack?' and the old Daddy shaky-shanks soon told him humbly, 'I want you, Master, to help me to get this here load upon my back.'"

This life-loving Powys stands in the

great line of romantic writers who died
abroad of consumption, a noble line which
includes Keats, Stevenson, Mansfield, and
Lawrence, but his work is neither febrile
nor morbid. He was a yea-sayer, finding
his own religion within him, like a good
Quaker, opposed to dogma and idolatry;
and as he lay dying he asked for pen and
paper, and he wrote:

"Now that I feel the hands of death
eager to get hold of me, now that my mor-
tal ears hear his tread under the slow-
growing red pines, now that I know him
to be standing in the road, under the rowan
tree, on the doorstep of the stoop, at cloaked
pause in the shadows of the weaving room,
the deep secrets that have been given me
to understand in my life of fifty-five years
are more than ever sustaining and I know
strong in my nature the unquenchable value of the ancient tradition of thought that
I have tried so sturdily to revive. This then
is my last word to the men and women, to
the boys and girls, and even to the little
children that I always so loved. Love life!
Love every moment of life that you experience *without pain*. Now that my hours so
sharply shorten (and I never was dull to
passing moments) I look back to the most
inconsequential and accidental of them
with the liveliest regret and yearning *to
have them again*."

Malcolm Elwin's *Life of Llewelyn*

Powys (John Lane, 1946) is a model biography, unpedantic, well proportioned, intimate though not gossipy, and solidly documented with chronology, genealogy, bibliography, and index. It is good to know that Powys is not without publisher in his own country, even though ours have written him off as a bad risk and our public forgotten him.

Literature has always been kept alive by a roomful of readers, and I am sure that Llewelyn Powys will never lack them, as long as his books sojourn in shops and harbor in libraries. He will speak to them right joyfully, as he did in his last postcard: "I shall be delighted, my dear John Rowland, to be associated with anything you write, whether of roguery, poetry, or philosophy. I believe with you that the present desolations will pass, and you and your children will live in a better age with simplicity and gaiety. Dust is soft, secret, and silent. I am not so well, but have had a happy life for half a century in sunshine— Bless you."

Islands of Books

MIDSUMMER in Southern California. How the sun hammers the earth, and the old jade responds with the ardent blossoms of hibiscus, geranium, and oleander! Fog in the early morning melts before noon, and the day walks naked, until sundown veils her in shadow. I sit at midday in my swallow's-nest study, reading, writing, and sweating, and my dreams are of rain forests and river gods. On the wall a colored print of Botticelli's Venus Anadyomene makes me yearn for a myth-begirt body of water. This land is too young for myths and poetry. The Indians were merely squalid, and their myths lack nobility and imagination. The Spaniards transplanted the Christian legend which never flourished, and has now withered away. And the Yankees sought only material gain.

What Jeffers wrote of the Carmel country is also true of this southern land: "The soil that I dig here to plant trees or lay foundation-stones is full of Indian leavings, sea-shells and flint scrapers; and the crack-voiced church-bells that we hear in the evening were hung in their tower when this was Spanish country. Where not only generations but races, too, drizzle away so fast, one wonders the more urgently what it is for, and whether this beautiful earth is amused or sorry at the procession of her possessors."

My imagination has always been fired by sight of our coastal islands, from San Miguel to San Clemente. Seen from Laguna Beach at twilight, sometimes the twenty miles of channel are smooth and small as a millpond, and Santa Catalina is like a purple shell, close enough to reach in a Gulliver-stride. Or coming over the Malibus from Seminole Springs one suddenly sees the fog-bound ocean like a bed of cotton batting, out of which rises the blue cone of Santa Barbara Rock.

I cannot free myself of the foolish thought of these sea-scattered islands as secret kingdoms, Hesperides - orcharded with golden apples, peopled with Bali-breasted women, or harboring Hebridean communities of crofters and fishers, as islands layered with legend, heavy with lore.

Alas, the truth is as dry as the islands' springs this summer after the long drought. San Clemente is a navy target area. Begummed by Wrigley, Santa Catalina suffers the ulcer of a resort town. Anacapa erects a necessary government lighthouse. Santa Cruz and Santa Rosa are pastured (in wet seasons) by cattle and sheep and highbooted herdsmen. Only remote San Nicolas offers its meager legend of the lost Indian woman.

Except for the Robinsons' charming booklet on one of the islands, there has been no adequate guide to them since Holder's book in 1910. No poetry, no patina of love and death and tears. The imagination hungers for such excitements as the death of Juan Rodriguez Cabrillo on San Miguel in 1543 and the location of his unmarked grave—our poor, faraway discoverer whose bleached bones were long since blown to oblivion.

Prior to Jeffers I know of only one writer about the California coast whose prose reaches poetical heights. Dana's descriptions of albatross, iceberg, ship sails, and the roadstead at Santa Barbara are to me utterly satisfying. "I shall never forget the impression which our first landing on the beach of California made upon me," he wrote in *Two Years Before the Mast*. "The sun had just gone down; it was getting dusky; the damp night-wind was beginning to blow, and the heavy swell of the Pacific was setting in, and breaking in loud and high 'combers' upon the beach. . . . We lay on our oars in the swell, just outside the surf, waiting for a good chance to run in. . . . We looked back and saw the ship . . . the Ayacucho, sharp upon the wind, cutting through the head seas like a knife, with her raking masts, and her sharp bows running up like the head of a greyhound. It was a beautiful sight. She was like a bird which has been frightened and had spread her wings in flight."

And yet one must have island books to read, to use for escape from chaparral lands too dry to feed the spirit. And so I have gathered on the shelf at my elbow a few Mediterraneans to muse about.

Here is Melville's *Journal Up the Straits*, which remained in manuscript for 74 years, after the author wrote it in 1857. His family, worried about the profound depression which followed the creation of *Moby Dick*, greatest of all ocean books, sent Melville on a solitary trip to the Near East. He visited Hawthorne en route, and our consul at Liverpool left in his journal a poignant account of their last encounter.

Melville's travel notes are fragmentary jottings without literary pretensions, yet they give a marvelous insight into the mind and heart of a great writer who found no public response in his lifetime to what he wanted most to write. They range from Constantinople to the Holy Land, Egypt and Italy. Here is a sample entry:

"Went towards the cemeteries of Pera. Great resort on summer evenings. Bank of the Bosphorous—like Brooklyn heights. From one point a superb view of Sea of

Marmora & Prince Isles & Scutari.—Armenian funerals winding through the streets. Coffin covered with flowers borne on a bier. Wax candles burn on each side in daylight. Boys & men chanting alternately. Striking effect, winding through the narrow lanes.—Saw a burial. Armenian. Juggling & incantations of the priests —making signs &c.—Nearby, saw a woman over a new grave—no grass on it yet. Such abandonment of misery! Called to the dead, put her head down as close to it as possible; as if calling down a hatchway into a cellar; besought—'Why don't you speak to me? My God!—It is I! Ah,—speak —but one word!'—All deaf.—So much for consolation. — This woman & her cries haunt me horribly.—"

Of the thousands of books about Egypt I presently cherish only one—Robin Fedden's *Land of Egypt*, published in 1939 by Batsford-Scribner. It is a poet's exact book about the people and the monuments, the geography, the history and the weather, and, above all, about the Nile, the country's sole *raison d'être*.

Venus Anadyomene—born of the sea foam—legendarily came to shore upon the island of Cyprus. I have a recent book about this tiny island off the coast of Palestine, Laurie Lee's *We Made a Film in Cyprus*, the journal of a young English poet who wrote the script for a government documentary about the island. It is a book of simple honesty and beauty, illustrated with stills from the film, and compresses within a few chapters an intense vision of a legend-heavy land of ancient culture.

For twenty years I have owned *Sea & Sardinia*, Lawrence's laconic travel masterpiece, and it remains one of my favorite Mediterraneans. My copy is the American edition published in 1921 by Thomas Seltzer, a small quarto illustrated from bright paintings by Jan Juta. It is very characteristic of Lawrence, a mixture of impressionism and exact observation of places and people, the chronicle of a brief winter journey by boat from Palermo, across Sardinia by railroad and motorbus, and back over the sea to Naples. Lawrence was extraordinarily responsive to the *genius loci*, wherever he went on his "savage pilgrimage" from Nottingham to New Mexico. Written at the zenith of his creative powers, this Sardinia book is quick with the sights, smells, and weathers of the mountainous island, and is seasoned by Lawrence's own wry reactions to the peasants along the way.

Norman Douglas is the author of some wonderful Mediterraneans: *Fountains in the Sand* and *Old Calabria* are my favorites: but I am hoarding notes on his books for a separate essay yet to be written. And there is Henry Miller's lyric book about

Greece, *The Colossus of Maroussi*, to which
I hope someday to pay tribute. Books on
the Riviera, Majorca, Provence, Spain, and
Mauretania, I have collected in modest
numbers, none of which, however, presently please me as much as a single volume
about the island of Corfu.

Prospero's Cell by Lawrence Durrell
was published only a few years ago by
Faber, and has not appeared in American
edition. The author is a young English-
man, born in Himalayan India, classically
schooled in England, who, instead of going
on to university in Cambridge, "ran away
to Europe." In the early 1930's he free-
lanced in Paris, and published a novel
called *The Black Book*, which gained him
an underground reputation. By 1936 he
was living in Corfu, and influenced by
South Wind wrote a novel called *Panic
Spring*, which was published pseudony-
mously (Charles Norden) in London and
New York. The war drove him to Greece,
Crete, and Egypt, and in the latter country
he spent four years as a British information officer, and as one of an extraordinary
coterie of literary exiles which included
Bernard Spencer, Terence Tiller, and Robin Fedden. Thence to Rhodes on a similar
assignment, to Argentina, where he lec-
tured for the British Council, and next to
Belgrade where he is now with H.M. Foreign Service. My printer friend Reuben

Pearson made me a small reprint of a nostalgic vignette of Corfu, written after Durrell's escape, called *A Landmark Gone*.

Faber has also published three volumes of his poems, and a verse play called *Sappho*; a brilliant novel about Crete has recently been issued in London, and Durrell writes me of a dozen other literary projects under way. His poetry is at once learned and lyrical, complex yet comprehensible, subtly dissonant, and (for me) habit-forming. As a poetical geographer he sees the isles of Greece:

> On charts they fall like lace,
> Islands consuming in a sea
> Born dense with its own blue:
> And like repairing mirrors holding up
> Small towns and trees and rivers
> To the still air, the lovely air:
> From the clear side of springing Time,
> In clement places where the windmills ride,
> Turning over gray springs in Mykonos,
> In shadows with a gesture of content.

Prospero's Cell, subtitled "A guide to the landscape and manners of the island of Corcyra," is a rich blend of history, conjecture, folklore, people and poetic insight. The title derives from a local belief that Corfu was the setting envisioned by Shakespeare for *The Tempest*. Durrell is a scholar as well as a poet, a connoisseur of people and places. His book is illustrated from drawings of Corfu made a century ago by

Edward Lear. The citron binding, the collotype plates, the tall, thin octavo size, the pleasing layout on cream stock, the feel, the weight, sight, and smell of the book, and the modest price of 10/6, all make it an apt example of why I prefer English format to American.

There are chapters on the local gods, folk dances, the puppet theater, Homeric vestiges (legend has Nausicaa a Corcyran), on the olive pressing and the vintage. Durrell ends his account of the olives by observing that "The whole Mediterranean—the sculptures, the palms, the gold beads, the bearded heroes, the wine, the ideas, the ships, the moonlight, the winged gorgons, the bronze men, the philosophers—all of it seems to rise in the sour, pungent taste of these black olives between the teeth. A taste older than meat, older than wine. A taste as old as cold water."

Night has fallen. It is time to end these notes. The music is *El Amor Brujo*. The food black figs, bread and honey. The drink cold water. Mediterraneans all!

My Melville

SHE IS la Reina de Los Angeles or plain Queen of the Cow Counties, depending on whether one is southside or northside of the Tehachapis; yet I, who have known her all the years of my life, must deny her rank with the world's great cities, for the reason that she lacks a body of water. Distant twenty miles the Pacific has never brought her more than money, and fog. By its influence water gives soul to a city. Whether it be river, lake, or ocean, water touching earth, where people swarm, works magic. London, Paris, Florence, Budapest, Istanbul. New York, New Orleans, San Francisco, Seattle. Yes!

Los Angeles? No! Filled and forgotten are the *zanjas*. The city's river is bedded with concrete, on which no myths accrete. Plenty of water in the pipes, tasting of chlorine and hard as flint, or boiled and bottled by Puritas. Take your choice. Rain water in the gutters, there today, gone tomorrow. A fountain or two. But no wind-dimpled body or turbulent flow. Absence of soul-bestowing water.

Even our harbor of San Pedro is synthetic, mechanized, and heartless. Tankered oil, tinned fish, cut lumber, and cased fruit. No waterfront swarm of indigenous sailors. No color. Ubiquitous stench of cooked petroleum, instead of the incense of roasting coffee that permeates the Embarcadero.

And so that summer day, as the motor ship *Orégon* nosed down channel from Terminal Island, my gaze from where I stood on the poopdeck overleaped the harborfront and sought that natural phenomenon which gives character and nourishment to the city: the barrier range of mother mountains, and particularly the westernmost San Gabriels, beneath whose blue bulk I was raised. They were my last sight of home, growing smaller and still tinier, like a row of jagged blocks on the horizon; and when I could no longer see them I walked forward to my cabin, opened my book bag and began to read, for the first time, *Moby Dick*.

There I was, supposedly well educated and I had never read Melville. Herman Melville! the man who, in the ensuing twenty years, I have come to respect, to cherish, yea, to love "this side idolatry." Alongside his rich experience, nobility of person, and the passion of his style, how cautious seems Emerson, how tricky Poe, Hawthorne anemic, and Whitman how posed!

Good fortune has attended my first reading of some books: *Ulysses* in Florence, *The Lands of the Sun* in rainy Paris, and *Moby Dick* on a month-long sea voyage to France via Panama. Here indeed were the time and the place and the book all perfectly conjoined.

My college course in American literature was given by a New Englander who carefully by-passed Melville. It was a Frenchman who brought our literature to life for me; a professor of English in Dijon's Lycée Carnot—the boys' high school —a stocky Burgundian who knew Americana from Wigglesworth to Wolfe. Jean Matruchot was his name, and with him I exchanged bilingual conversations three hours a week for more than two years; not in the classroom, but in the café—de la Comédie, de l'Union, de la Concorde, here and there about town where our fancy led, lubricating our talk with sips of the town's white wine colored with cassis; or sometimes in his rooms, which resembled a bookshop after an earthquake.

We became friends. He was twenty years older than I. Scarlet fever in his youth had left him nearly blind, and to read he had to hold the page an inch from his eyes. His life was full of tragedy. On the last day of the first World War his younger brother, who had been apprenticed to Rodin, was blown to pieces by a direct shell hit. Matruchot said I resembled his brother. I wore a beard in those years, and looked more French than American.

"Have you read *Moby Dick?*" I once asked Matruchot, soon after we became acquainted.

"*Nom d'un nom!*" he exploded. "And long before your Weaver and Mumford 'discovered' him!"

It was true. Matruchot gave me an essay he had written on Melville during his prewar student days at the Sorbonne. That and the books he lent me were my critical introduction to Melville. Jean Matruchot died in 1948. I write these lines in his memory.

The works of great writers have many uses. They educate the young, cement friendships, or lie placidly as reservoirs to which a man in need can return again and again at different stages in his life.

Such have been the works of Melville to me. I have never deliberately collected his books, and yet when these notes began to form in my mind and I summoned my Melvilles, they totaled nearly twenty. The cornerstone is of course *Moby Dick*, in the faded green Modern Library edition. Oxford's World Classics, best of all reprints, include *Moby Dick*, *Typee*, *Omoo*, and *White Jacket*. Another *Moby Dick* is in the Modern Library Giant edition, whose illustrations are to me Rockwell Kent's best work. And still one more version of "The Whale," in the text edition published by Oxford, edited by Willard Thorp, and illustrated from early whaling prints.

My finely printed Melvilles include the Grabhorn *Encantadas*, the Nonesuch *Benito Cereno*, and the Pynson *Journal Up the Straits*, about which I wrote in "Islands of Books."

Melville as diarist is particularly dear to me, for his entries are the man himself, entirely unself-conscious, writing for himself at the moment, with no posturing for posterity. In addition to the Near East journal there had been published (in the *New England Quarterly*) only a brief diary of Melville's 1860 voyage to California, until there appeared last year the *Journal of a Visit to London and the Continent, 1849-50*, edited by his granddaughter. Here is a typical entry, written a century ago:

"After dinner walked out to the lower walls and into the country along the battlements. The town is walled entirely. At dinner I drank nothing but Moselle wine —thus keeping the counsel of the 'Governor of Coney Island' whose maxim it is, 'to drink the wine of the country in which you may be travelling.' Thus at Cologne on the banks of the Rhine, and looking at the river through the window opposite me—what could I imbibe but Rhenish? And *now*, at Coblenz—at the precise junction of the

Moselle—what regale myself with but Moselle? The wine is bluish—at least *tinged* with blue—and seems a part of the river after which it is called. At dusk I found myself standing in the silence at the point where the two storied old rivers meet. Opposite was the frowning fortress—and some 4000 miles was America and Lizzie. Tomorrow I am *homeward-bound*! Hurrah and three cheers!"

Melville relished wine, rare beef, books, and friendly talk. His life divides neatly into periods of youthful adventure; popular success as the author of South Sea idyls; the philosophical and creative maturity of *Moby Dick*; repudiation of popular fame when he realized what the public demanded from writers; two decades of obscurity as a New York customs inspector; the final years of retirement with his wife, his books and his poetry, and the serene resignation of his last novel, *Billy Budd*.

I have saved till last the Melville to which I oftenest turn—an unpretentious little blue-cloth-bound book of 437 pages in the American Book Company's American Writers series, which cost new all of $1.55. It is "Representative Selections, with Introduction, Bibliography and Notes" by Willard Thorp. Of all the essential Melville which it contains, the quintessence is the series of confessional letters which Melville wrote to Hawthorne, at the creative zenith which he reached in the writing of *Moby Dick*. Time and again I have read these exalted letters from friend to friend, and their music was in my head when I spent an evening with the Rosenbachs in their Philadelphia home and the Doctor handed me what seemed to me the most precious book I had ever held: Hawthorne's own dedication copy of *Moby Dick*. I thought of them again on the summer day when Fred Adams and I drove through the Berkshires to Pittsfield, and found "Arrowhead," where Melville lived from 1850 to 1863, and where he wrote *Moby Dick* and the letters to his Lenox neighbor. The grass was on fire with goldenrod, and up valley to the north Melville's beloved mountain, Graylock, still filled the sky. "I have written a wicked book," he exulted, "and feel as spotless as the lamb!"

Thus does experience document reading, and reading heighten experience. Ever again the old saying holds true, that next to mother's milk books are the best food.

Leaves of Whitman

AFTER A PERUSAL of the new Everyman edition of *Leaves of Grass* I find myself eager to pay grateful tribute to old Walt, dead now this more than half-century. Mine is no Whitman collection in a bibliographical sense, and yet I have enough editions of *Leaves* to lead a non-collecting friend to ask, "Why do you have so many copies of the same book?"

Why do I? Because it is a book I love, and just as we like to see our beloved in different clothes, so does a favorite book gain charm in varied dress. The cornerstone of my Whitmans is the familiar Small, Maynard edition, in green cloth with gold flowering-grasses stamped on the spine. It bears my father's bookplate and an inscription to him in my mother's hand, dated Christmas, 1904, at Washington, D. C., two years before I arrived in the capital. I can remember my boyhood wonder at the title, *Leaves of Grass*. What did it mean? One never thought of a lawn of grass as having leaves!

This copy came to me when I was a senior in college, and I added my name beneath my father's, and the year 1928, and later I carried it around Europe with me as one of the few indispensable books.

At Dijon in 1931 I bought the first Everyman edition (1912) because it contained the long essay "Democratic Vistas." One of my subsidiary theses at the university was on Whitman's concept of the Pacific coast, and I used this copy for annotations.

While on a trip to England in the same year I picked up in a Charing Cross Road shop a copy of *Specimen Days in America*, the revised English edition of 1887. This rambling collection of journal entries about places and people has never grown stale for me. It ranks not far below Thoreau's journals of the seasons. *Specimen Days* appeared in 1931 in the World's Classics, but it was not until 1944 that I discovered this edition. It traveled with me on a flight to Seattle, and I can report that it reads well at 17,000 feet.

It was also in 1944 that I acquired my first edition (1855) of *Leaves*—in facsimile. For the price of $2 the Facsimile Text Society in 1939 reproduced the Lenox Library copy, with notes by Clifton J. Furness. An earlier facsimile edition was done by Mosher for the centenary in 1919, a book which today fetches at least $25.

As Whitman aged he kept revising and enlarging *Leaves*, until by the time of his death in 1892, the thin quarto of 1855 had grown fat, if not respectable. The new Everyman edition (1947), edited by Emory Holloway (the 1912 edition was edited by Horace Traubel), is the most complete text yet published. The poems are dated to show their first appearance and final revision. This edition contains no prose.

As a gift from Charles K. Adams came my copy of the Nonesuch Whitman, also edited by Holloway, which comprises complete poems and selected prose and letters. I own a 1914 *Complete Prose Works*, a compact volume of 527 pages. The Viking Portable Whitman, edited in 1945 by Mark van Doren, is selected poetry and prose.

In Gregg Anderson's *Recollections of the Grabhorn Press* he tells of the printing of the great folio *Leaves* ("400 copies printed and the press destroyed"), a book which today brings more than the published price of one hundred dollars. The 1940 Modern Library Giant *Leaves* is a photographic reproduction, reduced in size of course, of this monumental Grabhorn edition. The woodcut illustrations by Valenti Angelo are simple and beautiful.

Boardman Robinson was the artist for the Illustrated Modern Library edition (1944), a book which has one or two good pictures, but mostly leaves me indifferent. Shoddy manufacture is partly to blame. I also have the Rockwell Kent edition, printed in 1936 by the Lakeside Press in an inexpensive edition for Heritage. Kent's drawings of *things* please me more than his renderings of *people*. He has a way of making them all look alike — Elizabethans, Greenlanders, Faustians, Tierra del Fuegans, et al.

Edward Weston's photographic illustrations of *Leaves*, done for the Limited Editions Club, are another matter. I covet this edition.

As for books about Whitman, I do not collect them, contenting myself with reading library copies, from the one in 1867 by John Burroughs to Canby's most recent in 1943. Most of them are exhibitions of axgrinding, for Whitman stirs people to strong reactions. The richest source of information about the poet is Horace Traubel's *With Walt Whitman in Camden* (3 vols., 1906-1914), a Boswellian omnium gatherum, which has become uncommon and expensive. In anticipating his biographers Whitman left these lines:

When I read the book, the biography famous,
And is this then (said I) what the author calls
  a man's life?
And so will some one when I am dead and gone
  write my life?
(As if any man really knew aught of my life,
Why even myself I often think how little or
  nothing of my real life,

Only a few hints, a few diffused faint clews
   and indirections
I seek for my own use to trace out here.)

The one book about Whitman which I
own is one of the best, in that it uses few
words to say many true things. It is also a
beautiful book, set in Eric Gill's Monotype
Perpetua and printed on Arak ash-white
paper. This is Haniel Long's *Walt Whitman and the Springs of Courage* (Santa Fé,
Writers Editions, 1938). Most trade editions have become so ugly to sight and
touch, that I am thankful to this regional
press for producing a fine book at a fair
price.

Such then is my Whitman collection, a
few volumes gathered by inheritance, gift,
and purchase through two decades, read
and reread from youth to middle age, their
poetry still fresh and full of sustenance, as
in these lines:

I bequeath myself to the dirt to grow from the
   grass I love,
If you want me again look for me under your
   boot soles.
You will hardly know who I am or what I
   mean,
But I shall be good health to you nevertheless
And filter and fibre your blood.

San Joaquin

IT WAS AN English writer on America who said that California's interior is divided into three valleys: the Sacramento, the San Joaquin, and the Great Central Valley. England has no monopoly on provincialism; there are people in San Francisco who think "The Valley" means that little vineyard-grown backwater called the Napa; San Joséans refer to the prune-filled Santa Clara as "The Valley"; while down Hollywood-way a corral of stucco houses and station wagons known as the San Fernando rates local headlines as "The Valley." And well known is Steinbeck's impudence in titling a book of stories *The Long Valley*, when everyone but the eastern reviewers knew that it was the stubby Salinas he was writing of.

Who am I, an adopted southern Californian, to venture across the mountains and write about the southern half of the Great Central Valley? And yet it is often the foreigner who sees more and clearer than the native, who tends to become insensitive to his quotidian environment, his eyes to grow cataracts. Man should live instead by a constantly renewed vision, a process in which traveling and reading are necessary components. In writing of what I have seen and read of the San Joaquin I return some of the treasure I have found north of Tehachapi.

The finding took years. The San Joaquin does not give itself quickly to the stranger. It is goddess-like in requiring long propitiation before yielding. In this austere aloofness the Valley is the opposite of the dramatic coast at Carmel which can be had for a look. Witness Robinson Jeffers' response upon discovering Carmel in 1914: "When the stage-coach topped the hill from Monterey, and we looked down through pines and sea-fogs on Carmel, it was evident that we had come without knowing it to our inevitable place." The Valley cannot be had in that way. It is too long and too wide, too hazy in summer, too foggy in winter.

I recall my first flight over the Valley: at twilight from 17,000 feet the earth was checkered and shadowy. The neons of Fresno were rubies and amber. From forest fires in the foothills smoke spread for miles in lavender layers, sinister and beautiful. The old approach from Lebec via the Grapevine was dramatic, whereas the new highway drops one down like a millrace, the diesel taking the hindmost. Of all the Valley approaches I have made over the past thirty years, perhaps the most memorable was by auto from over the Sierra Nevada one September, after several years' absence from California, when the bleached blond hills near Sacramento were a relief from the monotonous green landscapes of the East.

There is no more dramatic Valley approach in literature than that of the Joad family. It is no poetic rhapsody, false to local topography. Recall the passage in *The Grapes of Wrath*, when the Joads have crossed the desert in their overloaded truck, bearing the dead body of Grandma, and reach their promised land at dawn:

They drove through Tehachapi in the morning glow, and the sun came up behind them, and then—suddenly they saw the great valley below them. Al jammed on the brake and stopped in the middle of the road. "Look," he said. The vineyards, the orchards, the great flat valley, green and beautiful, and the trees set in rows, and the farm houses.

And Pa said, "God Almighty!" The distant cities, the little towns in the orchard land, and the morning sun, golden on the valley. A car honked behind them. Al pulled to the side of the road and parked.

"I want to look at her." The grain fields golden in the morning and the willow lines, the eucalyptus trees in rows. . . .

I have lived in the Valley. For two summers when I was a boy I worked as a ranch hand near the Weed Patch, on the vast Di Giorgio acres between Edison and Arvin, when they were first being reclaimed from desert by irrigation. I know how hot the Valley can be. There was a recording thermometer outside the bunkhouse, and between noon and two o'clock the red line on the cylinder leveled off at 120 degrees!

I never cross the southern end of the Valley without remembering some detail of those two glorious blast-furnace summers. My first job was as waterboy to a gang of Mexicans tying grapevines. My task was to carry two skin-bags to the nearest flowing standpipe, fill them, and trudge back through the sand to where the men were concentrated; then I would pass along the rows giving out drinks to the thirsty laborers. "Agua, muchacho!" they would call. Down their open throats went gallons of water, while their Adam's apples bobbed. "Gracias!" and their teeth would flash. "Mucho calor," they laughed, mopping their faces and necks. From them I learned how to soak a bandana in water, place it on my head under the straw hat and let it hang partly down my neck.

I liked irrigating best, for it meant being alone in the midst of what was apparently a sandy wilderness. Sand is a devil when one is trying to stop runaway water with it. The water came from deep wells, clear and cold, and one could bury his face in a brimming standpipe and all but inhale the life-saving stuff. Now and then a truck would pass en route to the packing shed, and the swampers would toss out melons to be cooled and eaten at leisure.

That was twenty-five years ago and the Di Giorgio acres were not yet tree-grown, which meant that I could see the foreman coming in his Ford roadster when he was still miles away, allowing time to get up from the shade of the tall standpipe and be shoveling like hell by the time he drove past.

My only regret now is that I did not spend my entire boyhood there in the Weed Patch, for I might have accumulated experiences enough to enable me to write a Kern County Tom Sawyer, instead of these few notes on two faraway summers.

For I am envious of the accomplishment of William Saroyan, the Fresno boy who more than made good. Saroyan is at his best when he is most local. There is a truth and a warmth and a glory about his boyhood stories of Fresno and roundabout. I recently reread his story "The Pomegranate Tree," which packs into a few pages many essences of the Valley. Let me recall the opening paragraphs:

My uncle Melik was just about the worst farmer that ever lived. He was too imaginative

and poetic for his own good. What he wanted
was beauty. He wanted to plant it and see it
grow. I myself planted over one hundred pomegranate trees for my uncle one year back there
in the good old days of poetry and youth in
the world. I drove a John Deere tractor too,
and so did my uncle. It was all pure aesthetics,
not agriculture. My uncle just liked the idea
of planting trees and watching them grow.

Only they wouldn't grow. It was on account
of the soil. The soil was desert soil. It was dry.
My uncle waved at the six hundred and eighty
acres of desert he had bought and he said in
the most poetic Armenian anybody ever
heard, Here in this awful desolation a garden
shall flower, fountains of cold water shall
bubble out of the earth, and all things of
beauty shall come into being.

Yes, sir, I said.

I was the first and only relative to see the
land he had bought. He knew I was a poet at
heart, and he believed I would understand the
magnificent impulse that was driving him to
glorious ruin.

The most terrifying feature of the Valley
is neither the heat nor the cold, but Highway 99. This long racetrack has claimed
more lives than any other Valley hazard.
My friend, a Valley surgeon, said war was
never like the Saturday night slaughter on
Highway 99.

The only book I know to be devoted entirely to Highway 99, and the monsters
which make it a place of peril, is Bezzer-

ides' *Long Haul*. This short novel by
another Fresno boy of foreign origin is not
a major work. It has less plot and development and characterization than even
Saroyan's, but it evokes the spirit of the
wildcat trucker and is a valuable contribution to the perilous folklore of the highway.

There are minor novels about other aspects of the Valley, such as Howard Baker's
Orange Valley; *First the Blade* and *House
of Cedar* by May Miller; and titles by Ruth
Comfort Mitchell.

The Valley has produced, however, only
two major works of fiction, Norris' *Octopus*
and Steinbeck's *The Grapes of Wrath*.
Neither was written by a Valley native or
resident, yet both are monuments to the
spirit of the San Joaquin; and both were
the result of passionate indignation over
human wrongs. Norris' was retrospective.
The Octopus, a novel of the settlers' strug-
gle against the Southern Pacific monopoly,
is not a perfect novel, and yet it is read today, a half-century after publication, for
the reason that it has a great theme and
some great episodes.

Norris took many liberties with Valley
topography. He barely knew Tulare County, where the novel is laid. Instead he
moved down a ranch and a mission from
San Benito County, which it not in the
Valley at all. And the eastern wall of

mountains is out of his ken. But there is no doubt that Frank Norris felt the great pull and power of the Valley, and *The Octopus* bears witness to his pagan joy in the fecund earth. In somewhat the same vein is Steinbeck's third novel, *To A God Unknown*, which has for its setting the tiny Coast Range valley of Jolon.

It is interesting to examine Steinbeck's development up to and since *The Grapes of Wrath*. Until its publication in 1939, "Salinas John" had written poetry and journalism, historical, mystical, comical and proletarian novels, all but one with a Monterey County setting. He kept strengthening his art, fitting himself by study and by practical experience for the opportunity which came to him in the plight of the migratory workers in the depression. It was a big theme and he was ready for it. Unlike Norris, who documented *The Octopus* from the files of the Mechanics' Library in San Francisco, Steinbeck lived his novel before writing it.

I was in correspondence with him that winter of 1936-37, when he was writing *The Grapes of Wrath*. He had made money, for the first time, from *Of Mice and Men* and had "hutched up," as he called it, in a house at Los Gatos; and there he worked himself sick writing his masterpiece. A series of postcards told of its progress and completion; and then he fell into a slump of success from which, in my opinion, he has never emerged.

Steinbeck is no longer a Californian. He wrote *The Wayward Bus*, it is said, in the windowless air-conditioned office of his publisher, and it has a synthetic flavor, an unnatural warmth. I hope his curve goes up again. Rockets never soar twice, though, without recharging. The tree withers when the taproot is cut.

The Grapes of Wrath, like *The Octopus*, is not a perfect work of art. Its flaws are obvious: certain stock characterizations, overly poetic passages, a one-sided social indignation, but also like *The Octopus* it is noble in its vision of the common people, and it is vivid and compelling in its documentation. The Valley setting is faithful to reality: the heat and the rain, the culture of peaches and cotton, the migrants' camps and jungles, and the dilapidated vehicles which Steinbeck knew and loved so well.

What about the poetry of the Valley? I have passed negative judgment on Steinbeck's poetical interlardings. He is no eagle-eyed Jeffers. His blood is too warm; it melts his words and they blur.

The finest poetical prose about the Valley is half a century old. It was written by Mary Austin, another writer who favored the southern end. She left the Valley for Carmel and Santa Fé and wrote many books before her death in 1934, but never did she write anything finer than *The Land of Little Rain*, *The Flock*, and *Lands of the Sun*. Mary Austin first settled near Bakersfield in 1888, long before oil and irrigation and Highway 99 had civilized the Valley. *The Flock* is a pastoral in praise of sheepherding, with an extraordinary chapter on the Rancho Tejon. Twenty-five years later Mary Austin returned to California, and traveled slowly up-Valley from the Kern to the Sacramento, making nostalgic notes on the changes wrought, by irrigation.

I have left to the last the true poetry of the Valley, and it will not take me long to close, for the San Joaquin has never been the Muse's darling. Perhaps it is too big for the poetic eye to see as a whole, or does not allow the leisurely life which most poets need. And yet the Valley has born and bred one poet known to me who has received national attention with the eastern publication of his work and the award of a Guggenheim Fellowship.

William Everson was born at Sacramento in 1912, reared in Selma and schooled in Fresno, a true son of the twin valleys. His first poems appeared in pamphlet form in 1935. Four years later Ward Ritchie printed his first book, called *San Joaquin*, and to which I was privileged to contribute a foreword. During the war he was confined in Civilian Public Service camps in Oregon, whence he issued several pamphlets of verse. Afterward he moved to Berkeley where he acquired a handpress and founded the Equinox Press on which he printed a limited edition of his own poems called *A Privacy of Speech*. Upon conversion to the Roman Catholic faith the nature of his poetry changed. In 1951 Everson was received into a Dominican order, and will work as printer and bookbinder in an Oakland college.

Everson is not a prolific poet. He has published less than a hundred short poems about the Valley, but because he has a wide and clear vision, and precision and compactness of utterance, these San Joaquin poems of his hold for me the quintessential truth about the Valley weather and crops, its monotonies and subdued splendors. For Everson grew to manhood in the vineyards and orchards, laid concrete pipe, was a sugar-tester in a cannery, and finally acquired his own vineyard, then lost it during the war. Only a Valley farmer who had seen his raisins ruined by early September rain could have written

Under the whisper we watched it come over,
The raisins heavy yet in the fields,
Half-dried, and rain a ruin, and we watched it,
Perceiving outside the borders of pain
Disaster draw over:
The mark of the pinch of the coming months.
There was above us the sheet of darkness,

Deadly, and being deadly, beautiful,
Destruction wide for the dreading eyes,
What was hardly of notice another month
Now burned on our sight;
And it rode us, blown in on the wind,
Above and beyond and the east closed under;
It let down the ruin of rain.

There would be no Valley if it were not
for the great eastern wall called the Sierra
Nevada. Neither Steinbeck, Norris, nor
Mary Austin does justice to the granite
range which some days is revealed in glory
and at other times is half veiled or totally
shrouded, but once seen is always there in
the mind's eye, even when hidden by
clouds. In a dozen lines Everson fixes this
truth forever:

East: the shut sky:
Those walls of the mountains hold sunrise
    and wind under their backs.
If you tread all day vineyard or orchard,
Or move in the weather on the brimming
    ditch,
Or throw grain, or scythe it down in the
    early heat,
Taken by flatness, your eye loving the long
    stretch and the good level,
You cannot shake it, the feeling of mountains,
    deep in the haze and over the cities.
The mass, the piled strength and tumultuous
    thunder of the peaks.
They are beyond us forever, in fog or storm or
    the flood of the sun, quiet and sure,

Back of this valley like an ancient dream in a
    man's mind,
That he cannot forget, nor hardly remember,
But it sleeps at the roots of his sight.

Here finally, is one other poem by this
Valley man, who I believe to be the most
gifted Californian poet since Jeffers: the
title-poem of his book called *San Joaquin*:

This valley after the storms can be beautiful
    beyond the telling,
Though our city-folk scorn it, cursing heat in
    the summer and drabness in winter,
And flee it—Yosemite and the sea.
They seek splendor: who would touch them
    must stun them;
The nerve that is dying needs thunder to
    rouse it.
I in the vineyard, in green-time and
    dead-time, come to it dearly,
And take nature neither freaked nor amazing,
But the secret shining, the soft indeterminate
    wonder.
I watch it morning and noon, the unutterable
    sundowns,
And love as the leaf does the bough.

Ripeness Is All

WINTER has come, and the bush of sweet basil, which in summer was a melliferous magnet, stands now a dry ruin. When crumbled, the florets emit tiny seeds and invisible fragrance. I keep some of them in my study, to remind me of the past, and of the future. In this wintry time rain veils the hills, and my room is desolate unless I plug in the heater; then in the thermal air the hanging *mobile* turns and turns, and is never still. Likewise my mind simmers over body-heat engendered by tea and honey.

For a renewed sense of life, in this season of death, I am reading the works of three old men, one eleven years dead at 73, the other two still alive at 80. Shakespeare said, "Man must endure his going hence, even as his coming hither. Ripeness is all." And when ripens a man's work? In his 35 years Mozart progressed from preciosity through exuberance to serenity, a cycle which took Beethoven 57 years to fulfill. Titian painted masterpieces on into his nineties, and Verdi's septuagenarian *Otello* and octogenarian *Falstaff* are his ripest fruits.

Yeats, Gide, and Bunin are the three old Nobel laureates who nourish me through this fruitless winter. It was Yeats who said, "Sex and the Dead are the only things that can interest a serious mind." We can, I think, substitute Life for Sex without doing him violence. These are the absolutes: beginning and end. Great art is concerned with such ultimates, not with intermediates. Fashions, politics, sports have no place in the abiding work of these men.

What I offer is no treatise, for I have yet to read all of these men's books; rather, some impressions which seem to be turning into convictions. Of Gide, for example, I have yet to read the novel that has been called his masterpiece, *The Counterfeiters*; and I must confess to finding abhorrent his homosexual predilections. His recently translated Journals are nevertheless fascinating, even though I am sure they have been deeply cut. I had never read his youthful *Nourritures Terrestres* until it was translated last year as *Fruits of the Earth*. Passages in this prose poem moved me profoundly, particularly those about North Africa; for that Mediterranean littoral, sheltered by Atlas Mountains from Sahara and jungle, lies along the same latitude as the land I call home.

It is, however, a little book by Gide of fifty pages, published four years ago, which I unreservedly praise as a masterpiece. Written in his seventies, Gide's *Theseus* recalls Beethoven's last quartet, the opus 135: terse, compact, laconic, yet charged to the utmost with profound and exalted meaning. Gide's Journals show that he bore the seed of this book for thirty years before it germinated and fructified. It is his refinement of the Theseus of legend and literature, of Plutarch and Racine, told in the first person by the hero in his old age; and it recreates the glories of ancient Crete, the excitement of the Minotaur and Ariadne's thread. The story is tangibly sensual in its precise details, down to earth in its philosophy, and it culminates in Theseus' crowning work, the founding of Athens. As well as being one of Gide's finest creations, I believe *Theseus* to be an artistic peak of the mid-century.

What of the Irishman W. B. Yeats? He was being anthologized when I wore diapers, and I was exposed to his poems and plays in college, but it was not until a year after his death, in 1939, that I really met the man behind the voice. In a bookstore I saw the volume *Letters on Poetry from W. B. Yeats to Dorothy Wellesley*, and it was the honey-colored binding that took my eye. In spite of long academic discipline, my approach to literature is still unsystematic and casual, and it was mere optical delight that led to a decade of joyful reading.

I found that Yeats wrote better poetry the older he grew. When he was young, he said, his Muse was old; now he was old but his Muse was young. He is one of the few poets in history (Shakespeare was another) whose last work is his best. The tautness of his phrases, the stark beauty, the sensual awareness, the simplicity he had never achieved in his florid youth, came to him in old age. "The poems I can write now," he said, "will go into the general memory." When he died at 73 it was not ridiculous for an obituary to say that "he died like Shelley at the height of his life and with half his work unwritten."

When I ask why it is that Yeats has come to mean so much to me the answer is several. First of all, the rich feeling for life which his work radiates feeds my own hunger for earthly fulfilment. Then, his absolute devotion to his work is inspiring. Such consecrated poets are rare in any age, particularly in ours when interest in poetry (as distinguished from verse) is slight. And finally, a toughness of spirit which carried him safely through the dreaming, drunken nineties, the crossfire of Anglo-Irish politics, and most dangerous of all, his own world-wide fame.

To collect Yeats is also a joy, for his publishing span is from 1887 to now, with more than two hundred items to be cast for, and except for his rare first work,

Mosada, none of them costly. To be complete one would have to acquire the Irish Parliamentary Debates for Yeats's speeches during his term as senator. The collector's best guide is Roth's catalog of a Yeats exhibition at Yale in the year of his death. Biographies and critiques are appearing now in increasing numbers. An edition of his letters is awaited, as well as a critical collection of his works in verse and prose.

Not until last year did I read Ivan Bunin for the first time, although I was aware of his important position in Russian literature, particularly since he won the Nobel Prize in 1933. And it was the work of his old age which stirred me to the point where I am tempted to master Russian, if only to read his poetical prose just as he wrote it.

Writers of the huge novel forms—Tolstoy, Dostoevski, Dickens, and Scott—have never moved me the way Bunin does with a book of short stories written between 1938 and 1944, after continuous years of post-revolutionary exile in France. Only one or two are stories of France; the others have Russian settings. And what a master he is of evoking the Slavic landscape of winter snow and summer rye, and of creating the ambience of love which flowers but once! *Dark Avenues* (London, John Lehmann, 1949) is the name of this volume of erotic stories, and in translating them Richard Hare opines that Bunin's place in literature will probably depend upon such brief forms rather than upon his social novels.

"More attention will be paid," Hare continues, "to his beautifully polished poetic prose and to his consummate mastery of the short story form. For in the short story Bunin's peculiar evocative gift, combined with his verbal economy and sureness of touch, find an absolutely appropriate medium. The realistic detail, which he piles up so lavishly, is seldom without inner relevance to each picture as a whole, and his detached mode of understatement often reveals a deep sense of the limits of all verbal expression."

Mark Twain once offered to provide readers of his novels who did not like descriptions of nature with a supplement which would include only those passages. In Bunin narration and landscape are fused and inseparable.

He walked with me last Christmas on country roads in Tehama County. Almonds and walnuts were bare, oaks poorly leafed. Crows trooped raucously to roost, while in the upper sky V's of geese pointed toward the treacherous haven of the hunter-lined Sacramento. A mile or two east of the village I reached a vantage point on the crest of a rocky hill, and saw nearby Lassen topped by a wisp of smoke; and then a hundred miles beyond, the incredible sight of Shasta, snow-rosy in the sunset. My vision of all this was doubly intense, for I saw with my eyes and with his.

Thanks to Alfred Knopf half a dozen of Bunin's books have been published in this country, in characteristic Dwiggins format, but none since the Nobel furor died down; and these ripest fruits in *Dark Avenues* are available only in England. Thanks to an able book-scout (name upon request) I have assembled his translated books, and am savoring them in backward chronological order, but I have not yet come to any which move me as deeply as his last stories do, although the autobiographical novel *The Well of Days* is a beautiful account of his childhood and youth in southern Russia.

The *mobile* is a wintry thing. Suspended by a thread from the ceiling, the bleached wing-bone of a pelican looses five more threads, which end in twigs. Twigs in turn drop threads on which hang tiny shells, sand-dollars, bony fragments, and the pterodactyl skull of a gopher. In the rising heat these airy relics of wood, shell, and bone slowly turn, even as the books of three old men turn in my simmering mind.

Books on the Land

No LAND is truly civilized until literature has encrusted it with lore. That to me is California's great lack. Its first hundred years have produced material monuments of adobe, gold, steel, and concrete, which crumble, rust, and wear before our eyes. How few though are what Yeats called the "monuments of unageing intellect," those works of prose and poetry whereby a land lives forever in spite of material decay. One reared on English literature, though he live all his life in the Antipodes, dwells in the land of Mary Webb as much as any Shropshire lad, in Hardy's Wessex, or in the Somerset and Dorset so lovingly celebrated in the essays of Llewelyn Powys.

Ever since I realized how much I love California by living out of state once for three years, I have gone up and down the land endlessly looking for native literature which, again to recall Yeats, though local in setting is infinitely translatable in meaning—and have not gone in vain. For there *are* titans in our midst. Robinson Jeffers, for example, who by nearly forty years' work in Carmel has given his name to that coast between Point Piños and Point Sur. It was through his poetry I first knew that country, and subsequent explorations of it revealed no phenomena that Jeffers had not already observed and celebrated with eyes at once microscopic and visionary. Even flights over the Santa Lucias spied out nothing undescribed in soaring passages in *Cawdor* and *The Women at Point Sur*.

The Great Valley, at least the San Joaquin end of it, has been uplifted into literature by Mary Austin, Frank Norris, William Saroyan, John Steinbeck, and William Everson. What of the foothills? The northern Sacramento? I do not know of any work of literature which evokes the spirit of the great northern Valley. My mind glows with memory of Christmas spent near Red Bluff. On long sundown walks along dirt roads, smelling the windsweet fragrance of burning oak, my ears tingling with cold, challenged by every farmhouse dog, I carried in my pocket a copy of Bunin's *The Well of Days*; and I wondered if some Tehama County lad is now growing up there in that river country, watched over by Lassen and Shasta, absorbing experience and destined some day to recreate it in strong and living prose, in the way the Russian did his Voronezh origins.

I did not know it then, but over the Siskiyous in the watery, wooded valley of the Willamette a young man was building a cabin, and with his wife mimeographing a booklet of his own poems. I received Don Emblen's *The Crow Tree* a month later, and on a trip to San Diego learned something about him from his former colleagues in the Public Library. In a nearby bookstore I found a copy of Don and Betty Emblen's earlier book of San Diego shoreline verse called *There Are Seagulls On Our Lawn*; and flying back to Los Angeles that night through rain-turbulent air, I experienced the further excitement of true poetry.

Deep in the valleyed mountains of the San Diego back country lives Judy van der Veer. My wife and I visited her last year, and with Judy and her niece Wowser we walked through the mountain lilac (beloved habitat of ticks) to a flat view rock, from where we looked over valleys and lesser mountains to Cuyamaca — Old Queer Mack — which stands shoulder to shoulder with his gang and dehydrates every passing cloud. Everything I saw that day was already known to me from reading *Brown Hills, November Grass*, and her other books, for Judy van der Veer has looked at San Diego county long and with love.

Another folk writer who has taken many counties for his own is Idwal Jones.

China Boy, Vermillion, and *Vines in the
Sun* are some of his best California books.
They are earthy works, enriched by passages such as this—"Some cedar-trash was
burning, charging the air with the sweet-
ness of pencilwood, and on the wind came
full the California winter smell, a com-
pound of earth and grass, tar weed and
anise, crumbled walnuts, the sharp rank-
ness of wild oranges, and the medicinal
tang of blue-gum leaves."

Our cities have not been as fortunate in
the literary treatment they have received.
Los Angeles is the hardest to write about,
because of its amorphous character. Its ex-
aggerated ways are easily satirized: witness *Ape and Essence* and *The Loved One.*
In his detective novels Raymond Chandler
comes closer to capturing the true *psyche*
of the Angel City.

Whereas San Francisco, in its beautifully naked peninsula position, should be an
easy mark for any sharp-eyed poet or wide-
eyed novelist. Yet I do not know of many
writers of what I judge to be lasting literature, who have become inseparably iden-
tified with San Francisco. Oscar Lewis is
one. His novel *I Remember Christine* has
real Franciscan flavor. Clarkson Crane is
another. Few novelists wait, as he did,
twenty-one years between their first and
second books. In 1925 Crane's *The Western
Shore* was one of the first, and remains one

of the best, novels about university life in
Berkeley. Two decades later he published
in rapid succession two powerful San Francisco and Bay region novels, *Mother and
Son* and *Naomi Martin*, which are apparently the opening movements of a Franciscan *comédie humaine*. Needless to say, in
the present jackpot state of publishing,
they are out of print and hard to find.

Ahead of us are ninety-six inscrutable
years before the Bicentennials begin. Perhaps in 2046 our descendants will have
substituted Norris, Jeffers, Steinbeck, Everson, Jones, van der Veer, Crane, and
others yet unborn, for those tired titans,
Twain, Harte, and Miller, whose western
works are in these centennial years more
praised than read. And the last adobe will
have returned to the mud, the bridges
sagged, the dams sprung leaks, and that
literary patina which means civilization
and culture have become several unre-
movable layers deeper.

Personal Landscape

SOUTH OF Tehachapi my personal landscape begins. Born in the District of Columbia, man without a state, I have taken this mostly dry and wrinkled land for my own; and the tendrils which boyhood rooted in the irrigated earth of the orange orchards have spread like serpents under the soil from Hemet to Hueneme; so that I am attached to the ground at all points and nourished the year round from subterranean sources.

It is now a landscape overrun by humanity avid for pleasure and profit, oil-smutched under smog veil, bright with the kleigs' false light, and bristling with the sterile antennae of television, all but unsung by creative folk as it collapses into industrialism; a drought-thirsty land whose soul craves the love offered only by artists. Raped repeatedly by writers come to milk the Hollywood cow, waughed at and huxleyed on, this myriad-swarming land of luckless loot still awaits her ode, her epic.

Once more under the hammer of summer, while girding to sail for an overseas sojourn, with Whitman, Melville, and Jeffers peopling my mind, I would praise my personal landscape, offer words of love and compassion, pledge her my faithful return, and the ultimate nourishment of my ashes.

This land of mountain and littoral, of orchard, vineyard and factory, fed by conduited water and power, was praised a generation ago by Mary Austin, Margaret Collier Graham, Amanda Mathews, Olive Percival, Charles Lummis, and others, in books now nearly forgotten. Then came the waves of immigrant locusts, stripping the leaf, sucking the juice, splitting the acre, playing mudpie with stucco and asphalt, comic-stripping in wind-tunnels, mish-mashing science, religion, and art to pastiche: small wonder the satirist flourished!

The people have prospered. I make no lament for them. My personal landscape it is I exalt; some gone, much doomed, a little destined to endure. Gone is my first green-growing world of the Rust Nursery in South Pasadena: great blocks-square lath-shaded land of Jap-watered seedling, plant and tree, obscure maze of secret adventure where facts of nature were nakedly revealed.

And west of town the squirrel-loud Monterey Hills, yielding toyon and mistletoe to be hawked at Christmas. Northward the old Raymond Hotel and links, now razed and converted to housing project. The mys-

terious manor on Bilicke Hill. Eastward
groves of orange and pomegranate, where
in gangs we fought and stole, reaching to
Huntington's bookish domain: keep out!
And coursing town the *zanja*, called sanky,
alternately open and covered, wherein
(apaches all) we played Sewers of Paris,
shocking the short-haired bourgeoisie. All
changed in reality; immortal in dream.

Personal landscape of town, mountain,
canyon, and plain, nearly tree-barren,
waterless, decontoured, subdivided to zero
prime, how few are we who have seen you
plain and remained eager to praise! There
have been notable painters: Wendt, Craig,
Zornes, Sheets, and Robinson; and sculp-
tors, though fewer, because commissions
for statues and fountains were scarce.

True poets are uncommon; one is Hilde-
garde Flanner of Altadena, mute for too
long. Another is C. F. McIntyre. With what
magical phrase he praised the biblio-pas-
toral life on the La Crescenta alluvial! His
sonnet "Drouth" speaks more than a shelf
of Southern Californiana:

Regard the withered buckthorn, dead deer-
    weed,
the rattling tambourines of lupine seed,
the motherly yucca wilting with full pods,
the moribund sagebrush mouthing earth's dry
    paps . . .
Then listen for the secret thoughtful rain

down-sifting slowly, slowly, in the laps
of drowsy harvest-gods:
Gods with gold faces whose breath is winnow-
    ing.
Here walks causality in its calm round, pre-
    paring epic deeds,
even this instant trickling of ripe seeds.
How each doom-bearer, deftly, with no sound
sinks, sure as a corpse into the burial ground,
ah, slyly winking, planning resurrection.

Twenty years have passed since he
taught me to scrape the stucco, x-ray the
asphalt, and ignore the neon mirage of
success. Two decades have gone since we
fought the brush-fire away from his book-
packed cabin, only to lose it to that Gren-
del-like flood which scoured the slope of
cabin and chaparral. His La Crescenta lyrics, mostly unpublished because he scorns
them for learned later work, are the im-
mortelles of that sage-sweet epoch, an en-
during Anthologia Californica.

There is the poet called Peter Lum
Quince (the Lum was added to the Shake-
spearean pseudonym to fill out a line of
type on a title-page) whose four fragile
volumes may outlive bulkier books of our
time. Did Aldrich not write

What mighty epics have been wrecked by
    Time
Since Herrick launched his cockle-shells of
    rhyme!

In *The Year's at the Spring*, issued in

1938 in an edition of 150 copies with wood-engravings by Paul Landacre, the flowering Quince offered eight lyrics to lost love, each enfolding a regionai blossom such as yucca, jacaranda, acacia, and pepper. Eleven years later Quince ripened again to bear another lyric suite, which he himself printed in only twenty-five copies, aptly called *A Few More*.

The Santa Monica range rises as the Hollywood hills, then runs seaward and forty miles up coast to an abrupt ending at Mugu. Mile after mile the settlers have wormed it with roads and scurfed it with stucco, as louder and angrier the voice of the bulldozer is heard in the land. The out-posted love nests have been cuckoo-swarmed into multiple dwellings. All has been mapped and made known.

For six years we dwelled in a canyon cleft of these mountains, and I came to love their seasonal ways. Rarely did the fog's fingers probe to our depth. Our music at night was the cry of coyote on the moony ridge trails, and in the gray dawn the lament of the mourning dove called rain-crow. Fox, skunk, and weasel sought the hen and her egg. War's end brought house-builders in nail-sharp hordes. We fled to the plain.

The literature of the Santa Monicas is as sparse as her trees. Writers are blinded by the city lights, deafened by sound effects, exhausted by the smoke from a million motors. If they lift their eyes to the hills, it is to the higher San Gabriels and San Bernardinos which together form the Sierra Madre. The Santa Monicas are too subtle to impress the stranger; superficially too dry and acrid to nourish those whose roots fail to reach the rain-filled reservoirs which rest on bed-rock.

Madeleine Ruthven wrote a pamphlet of poems, *Sondelius Came to the Mountain*, about the folklore of the canyons west of Malibu. Poet John Russell McCarthy was employed by a promoter to write a prose dithryamb to the Santa Monicas. The pitifully uprooted Christopher Isherwood scorned them in a diatribe on Los Angeles in the American number of *Horizon*.

There is fortunately one beautiful novel about boyhood, growth, and change in a canyon of the Santa Monicas. Peter Viertel's *The Canyon* was published ten years ago when the author was barely twenty years old. A chapter from the work in progress drew a "D" in a composition class at UCLA. The Library there now houses the entire manuscript of this novel and would not trade it for treasure. It opens:

"The cliffs follow the seashore in long curving lines, standing high over the water. They break in a few places, fall off, and form canyons that are cut deep into the brush-covered hills. They lead to the

Valley that lies behind the mountains, flat on its back, its fuzzy belly upward to the hot California sun."

The theme of Viertel's book is of a boy's progress through adolescence and tender sexual initiation to young manhood, and of the concurrent change of canyon from country to city. It is written in simple prose, with the quality of poetry, and is out of print and all but forgotten.

His personal landscape is mine. And there for me is the whole quest and end of literature: to find and to cherish those works whose vision merges with mine. So few are they in this local region that in my need I shall be compelled to fashion my own. For touchstone, landmark, and symbol, I shall survey the landscape south of Tehachapi and beyond, from high-spying plane, from car, and on foot, conscripting the peak of Jacinto whose monolithic bulk soars above smog; the limestone statue of Garcés, discoverer of the San Joaquin, which ennobles Bakersfield; such fabulous trees as the lemon-scented gum known as the Ellwood Queen at Goleta, the Moreton Bay fig in Santa Barbara, the cathedral camphor in Ontario; the sea-swallowed isles from Miguel to Clemente.

These are my heritage and joyful solace, my personal landscape. Them I bid hail and farewell!

Designed by Ward Ritchie, printed by
Fabe Litho, Tucson, and bound by
Roswell Bookbinding, Phoenix.
Credit is due to Dick Laws
and Rebecca Gaver
for help in production.